COME HOME

COME HOME

A CALL BACK TO FAITH

JAMES MACDONALD

MOODY PUBLISHERS
CHICAGO

© 2013 by
JAMES MACDONALD

Published in association with the literary agency of Wolgemuth and Associates, Inc.

Edited by Neil Wilson
Cover Design: Media Communications Department of Harvest Bible Chapel
Interior Design: Smartt Guys design
Cover Image: Shutterstock

Library of Congress Cataloging-in-Publication Data

MacDonald, James, 1960-
 Come home : a call back to faith / James MacDonald.
   pages cm
 Summary: "The prodigal. The wanderer. The skeptic. The rebel. Each of us knows someone who has walked away from God, and it is heartbreaking and bewildering. We wonder how to reach out to them and bring them back, but often it seems impossible. Maybe you yourself are the one who has walked away and sees little reason to return to faith and the church. The invitation of this book is this: come home. It invites the departed to return and offers the promise of the gospel - that all wrongs and sins can be forgiven through Jesus. There is no expiration on the promise of forgiveness and the open arms of Christ, so no matter how long the wanderer has wandered she is still welcome. All hurts can be healed, all brokenness mended. Just come home. Whether you are a family member or friend of the prodigal or whether you are that person, this book offers hope and an open invitation to return the safety of forgiveness and restoration in Jesus"-- Provided by publisher.
 Includes bibliographical references.
 ISBN 978-0-8024-5718-9 (hardback)
 1. Ex-church members. I. Title.
 BV4921.3.M27 2013
 248--dc23
                                 2013012816

We hope you enjoy this book from Moody Publishers. Our goal is to provide high-quality, thought-provoking books and products that connect truth to your real needs and challenges. For more information on other books and products written and produced from a biblical perspective, go to www.moodypublishers.com or write to:

Moody Publishers
820 N. LaSalle Boulevard
Chicago, IL 60610

3 5 7 9 10 8 6 4

Printed in the United States of America

Dedication

To all the wanderers I have known
(some of you know who you are)
whether or not you are home yet, we love you!

And to all who have taken to heart the challenge
to go get the wanderer.

My brothers,
if anyone among you wanders from the truth
and someone brings him back,
let him know that whoever brings back a sinner
from his wandering will save his soul from death
and will cover a multitude of sins.
James 5:19–20

CONTENTS

FOREWORD

I DON'T LIKE the word *prodigal*. It's not in the Bible and it doesn't describe me well. I was a wanderer. No doubt about it. A pastor's daughter from a loving family, but for a season I wandered far away. I knew better. I didn't have to, but it's part of my history now, a bad chapter in a good story with a grace ending. I didn't plan to wander. It hurts to remember that I did, but maybe my admission can call a wanderer home or help you love one until they do.

I didn't wake up one day and amble off. At no time did I decide to leave my family or my faith—it just happened, without my realizing, one step at a time. Hurt and stubborn, I stumbled along in adolescent secrecy to wherever my wandering feet took me. Drifting further and further, I lost sight of what I treasured. Frightened and alone, I became uncertain what "home" was or if it even existed for me. Looking back, I see how very confused I became, and this is the worst part—I didn't know it at the time.

The darkest part of wandering until you're lost is that you lose your sense of home and why it matters and how to get back. Blind to the road ahead and deaf to people who loved me, I was full of fear and couldn't read the road signs. Wanderers don't need anger over how they have hurt you; they won't hear your pleas and can't comprehend your reasons. But they are lost, and only your love and God's love through you can find and bring them home. Don't despair, no matter how far your wanderer gets. Looking back, it is truly a miracle of grace that I ever made it home, but thankfully I did. God will give you strength until your wanderer does, too.

Jesus said, "He who is forgiven much loves much," and by His grace I love my family and my Savior as only those who have wandered and come home can. Home is faith in Christ and family and the comfort of what is familiar. Home is truly where the heart is, and I am so thankful for the love that brought me home.

For those waiting for a wanderer to return, it's important to think of him or her as God does—loved and forgiven. Otherwise, when they do come home, you will drive them away again with your demand for answers. It's home at its best that they long for, and home at its worst they dread. Let God prepare your heart for the "robe-and-ring" welcome of the Father that Jesus talked about in Luke 15. In time you will learn a lot more about the wanderer's time in a far country. What is essential now is to let God prepare your heart for an unconditionally loving welcome.

If you are a wanderer reading this page now, I beg you to listen to those who have loved you longest and know you best. "Home" may seem scary to you, and maybe you can't imagine yourself there again, but home is who you really are and the only place you will experience lasting peace and happiness. People wander for real reasons, and in these pages I pray you find understanding about why you left home. I pray you find strength to admit where your life is not working. Most of all, I pray you find hope that what your heart is longing for is back at home, right now.

No matter where you are or what you have done, your Father in heaven loves you and wants to embrace you this moment with grace and forgiveness. Come home to Him. If He seems far away, if you're not sure you believe, run now to those you know, who know Him best. Did they give you this book in hopes that a conversation could begin? Read with an open mind. Its message may be a map for you. Even if you're not sure you want to know, even though it seems impossible now, people are praying for you, asking God to open your wandering heart to see where you've gone, that you'll awake to where you truly belong . . . and Come Home.

Abby—2013

INTRODUCTION

UNTIL IT IS A FATHER or brother or sister or son, you don't really know the pain of living with a wanderer. I didn't. I knew how to pray kneeling and out loud, but I didn't know what it was to pray in the night and see my tears falling on the carpet just inches from my face. Only a wanderer can get you to that awesome place of desperation—and to God meeting you in ways so powerful and personal you never dreamed were possible.

I preached the messages behind these chapters during the most difficult period of my life, and I can honestly say that when I have occasionally overheard the recordings in the production studio or randomly in my car on my favorite radio station, I have quickly shut it off or walked away. That being said, I am sure you can understand my reticence to put these messages in writing. I do so only because I have a story to tell of

God's faithfulness to Himself, to His Word, and to my family, in the hope He will do the same for you.

As I circulate among our own church family and travel to places around the world to preach God's Word, I encounter again and again people whose lives have been torn open by wandering loved ones who are searching for help and hope apart from Christ.

This is a book about those wanderers. They leave our families, our friendships, and our churches. As you will find, they come in both genders, many ages, and with unique experiences. But they also fall roughly into several categories worth knowing. The purpose of this book is to develop a greater heart for the hurting people we must not forget, to learn what we might do to bring them home, and to prepare a welcome for those we desperately miss and long to have beside us again.

Peter, Thomas, Samson, and the Prodigal Son are four wanderers we meet in the pages of the Bible. There are many more. But each of them represents a particular kind of wanderer God loves and wants to send a message to: Come Home.

No doubt you have a wanderer or two in your life. I wish I could tell you that God will use you personally to bring that person home. More often than not though, it seems God uses another to reach the ones most on our hearts. Too often in the lives of our own wanderers, we have been part of their struggle, a source of their pain, a barrier to their belief at some level. As you pray for God to bring someone into your wanderer's life to restore them, I challenge you to be that help for someone else.

All around you are people who used to love God, who once attended church but for some reason wandered off. God knows the reason and wants to use you in bringing them home. Pray for the wanderers most on your heart and go to work on the ones around you. My experience is that when we take care of what is on God's heart, He will take care of what is on ours. That's what I did in preaching these messages, and God honored that effort beyond even my prayers. Now I am praying that you will do the same. As God uses you to bring home a wanderer, you may just be surprised to hear from the one you love, so far from the Father's arms today.

Warmly in Christ our Savior,

James MacDonald

CHAPTER 1

GO GET THE
WANDERER

THERE IS NOTHING quite like seeing a verse in Scripture for the first time! I mean, maybe you've read it a hundred times, but suddenly one day, God's voice reaches your heart from those words and you are rocked to the core. Until that moment, the words made sense—now they are a scalpel that cuts right to the core. Such has been my experience recently with James 5:19–20 as these statements have grabbed my heart:

> **My brothers, if anyone among you wanders from the truth and someone brings him back, let him know that whoever brings back a sinner from his wandering will save his soul from death and will cover a multitude of sins.**

Those forty words are the foundation for this chapter and this book. Read the verses again, and let them sink in.

Before we look closely at this passage, let's take a cultural step back. Does that word *wanderer* ring any bells for you? We don't use it in common language. But in 1961, Dion, one of those single-name artists, recorded a song called "The Wanderer." If you're from my generation you can probably hear the song in your head. It got as high as #2 on the charts and is now listed in *Rolling Stone* magazine's list of *The 500 Greatest Songs of All Time* at position 239. In many ways, that song captures the adventure and danger in a wanderer's life. His life roams around and never settles down. His relationships are temporary. He doesn't really connect with where he is, where he's been, or where he is going. He is lost, wondering vaguely if there's something better, but caught in the not-so-merry-go-round of wandering. Unfortunately, if you are a wanderer, or have been one, it's hard to admit this is reality even in rare quiet moments of reflection.

There is a command expressed in the title of this chapter: "Go Get the Wanderer." From Jesus' parable of the shepherd who goes after the one lost sheep, to James' sober call to action, the message is the same: "Go get the wanderer! Go get them!" I'm going to be repeating the command a few more times in these pages.

I'm also going to try and motivate you to take action. Let's start with this reality—

THE PROBLEM EXISTS.

Men and women everywhere have a tendency to wander—even in the church. Sheep wander, even in the flock of the Good Shepherd. That's why James includes the problem in his practical letter to believers. The whole book of James is about growing up and going forward in your faith, getting to a place of maturity, and developing completeness as a disciple of Christ. Full-blown discipleship is what James is all about.

As he comes to the end of the book, James is talking about maturity expressed in praying for the sick. But not just anyone who is sick—praying specifically for the person who is sick because of sin. Is all sickness because of personal sin? No. Some people suffer sickness and hardship for the glory of God. When Jesus' disciples noticed a man who had spent his whole life blind they asked, **"'Who sinned, this man or his parents, that he was born blind?' Jesus answered, 'It was not that this man sinned, or his parents, but that the works of God might be displayed in him.'"**[1] They assumed only sin can explain sickness; Jesus knew better. Though it's not *always* because of sin, sometimes sickness *is* caused by sin. If you realize you are suffering because of your sin, you need to confess it and pray in faith. Ask others to pray for you. It's all there in James 5:16: **"Confess your sins to one another and pray for one another, that you may be healed."**[2] He then gave the example of Elijah who prayed for the healing of a land.[3] Unbelievable. Most books in the Bible close with a final greeting, "Say hi to so-and-so and keep in touch." Not this one. James ends his letter with a call to go get the people who have lost their way.

Let's take these two closing verses a phrase at a time. The expression, **"My brothers,"** aims to get our attention: "Now don't miss this *last* thing!" The song "The Wanderer" we mentioned earlier laments the tendency of all human beings to wander. However, James' real concern is not wandering people, but wandering Christians. He's calling on brothers to care for brothers. He wants sisters to look out for sisters. He's thinking about people who embrace the truth and then wander away from it. No doubt you're thinking of some who fit the wanderer category. Or maybe you realize someone has *you* in mind.

So when James reaches out and says, **"My brothers,"** what he's saying is, "Listen up! Go get the wanderers, my brothers, my sisters." Everyone's included in this. I wish we still used the word *brethren*; it seems kind of old-fashioned, but everyone understood that *brethren* meant *brothers and sisters*. No one's off the hook on this one. James is emphatic—"My brothers and sisters—family of God! Go get the wanderer!" Wandering was a problem then, and it is now. Going astray is a reality we have to deal with if we're really family; if we are truly brothers and sisters.

Notice James' next phrase, **"My brothers, if anyone among you."** Again, nonbelievers are not in view here. He's talking about people among us, folks who once were with us. These are fellow Christians you could probably think of right now. "They used to sit behind us in church. Where are they?" If you're typical, you probably sit in the same general location in the worship center and come to the same service each week. You could probably run a little inventory of the people you sit near. "So what happens if the people who used to sit beside me or near me disappear? I don't see them anymore. I haven't heard why sister so-and-so is missing. Should I notify someone?" It's very important that you find out what happened to them.

Think for a moment about this phrase: **"If *anyone* among you."**

You may find yourself asking, "Well, who are we talking about exactly by the term *wanderer*? Can you give me some examples?"

We surveyed 100 people and the Top Five Answers are on the board to this question: Name a kind of person who wanders.

(1) A prodigal wanderer.

This person's motto is, "You're not going to tell me! Nobody tells me what to do. I do what I want to do." Sometimes being a prodigal is related to being young and rebellious. Sometimes, though, it has nothing to do with age. You could be in your sixties, still be willful and stubborn, and say, "I want to do my thing, my way." This is the prodigal wanderer. "I'm following my own path!"

(2) The pleasure-seeker.

This person isn't willful, just selfish.

"I want what I want."

"Why are you doing that?"

"'Cause I *want* to!"

"Yeah, well those choices are going to hurt you."

"Well, I don't *care*! I do what I *want* to do because it feels good *now*."

This is the person who has found a particularly tempting sin. The Bible says **"the pleasures of sin"**[4] are for a season. They don't last. But this person says, "I'm going to enjoy myself. This makes me happy, and it's what I want to do. I'm having too much fun to worry about what's coming down the road." That's the profile of a pleasure-seeker. They're out there wandering. If you were to talk to them, they might be really nice about it. They're not willful like the prodigal, but their behavior is careless. You might ask, "Why don't you stop?"

"'Cause I don't want to, and I haven't heard a good reason why I should."

(3) The wounded wanderer.

Now if you talk to a wounded wanderer, he or she has a story. "I used to go to church. I used to love God. I used to study my Bible."

"What happened?"

Out comes the story, and it usually involves a person. Maybe it was a parent or a pastor or someone else who claimed to be in a place of spiritual authority. "People who I trusted failed me. They hurt, wounded, and disappointed me. I'm disillusioned now, so I'm not with God anymore." Though their pain is not because of God, but caused by the actions of another person or group, God may really be who they blame.

(4) The ashamed wanderer.

This person lives with a sense of shame over mistakes and

sins of the past. What happened to them? Galatians 6:1 says, **"If anyone is caught in any transgression . . ."** Sometimes sin seems to run you down and tackle you.

"I was going along, trying to live for God. But I've fallen, and I can't get up! I stumbled into something, and I can't go back to church. People know what happened to me! People realize what I did! I'm going to feel so ashamed. I can't *face* those people!" Sound familiar?

Part of what makes our church wonderful is that it's filled with people who understand life's detours. They know about shame and offer a very loving, safe place where broken people can come. That's because they were once broken themselves! They say, "*I* was that person at one time in my life. I was *ashamed* to go to church." For many in our church, that's our story. And most of us know someone who is far from the Lord today because they just can't face God's people. Have we tried to reach them?

Here's the last identifiable group of people we need to watch for:

(5) The distracted wanderer.

"Why aren't you at church today?"

"Well, I don't know. I couldn't tell you how or when, but God disappeared from my life."

Sometimes the distracted wanderers are even at church, but not really *there*! The lights are on, but no one's home. Their attention is somewhere else. The afternoon football game may not start for hours, but they are into the pregame show in their minds. Ask the distracted wanderer to come to church, and they say, "Sure! Where are we going for lunch afterwards?" They're not *on* task. They just don't get the point. They're not plugged in. They can listen to someone pouring out his heart about life with God, and their response is, "Yeah, I'm not seeing it."

You may have been that person. Your story is one sentence: "I just didn't get it!" Or maybe you know and love someone like that?

Now listen to me: Go get the wanderer! Track down that person. They're not going to come back without some help.

The problem of wanderers exists in the church. **"My brothers, if anyone among you . . ."** Notice it's *anyone*. You just have to stop and say, "This could be anyone." There are people who God's Spirit is going to bring to your mind while you are reading this. Has it already happened? Has someone's face unexpectedly popped into your mind? Guard yourself against the thought, "Oh, not him. Not her. They're too far gone. They're not coming back! I'll start with an easier one!" But no one is beyond the reach of God's grace. No one has gone so far that they are out of God's sight.

When the text says *anyone*, you can't say, "They're too far gone."

When God's Word says *anyone*, you can't say, "It's too complicated or too messy. I can't really get into that."

You can't make those excuses when God's Word says *anyone*.

James continues, **"My brothers, if anyone among you . . ."** Now the big word: **wanders.** The NASB says "strays." The Greek term actually is *planetai* from which we get our word *planet*. In New Testament times they obviously didn't have Google Maps or a GPS. Ancient people kept track of direction when they traveled by using the sun and stars. Early on, they included the planets as guides—problem! The planets changed location in the sky, so there were not great results. "When I used to follow that planet, I would get to Indiana, but now I end up in Minnesota." Planet tracking wasn't super reliable. The idea that the planets shifted—*planetai*—came to mean *something moving, wandering*. Here's a good definition: to wander is to proceed without a proper sense of direction. That's what wandering is—spinning out of orbit.

Planetai is the same Greek word used in Hebrews 11:38 regarding faithful people who were wandering without homes (but not without purpose!). The same expression appears in Matthew 18:12 when Jesus talked about people who were wandering like sheep without a shepherd. Jesus reflected the shepherd's heart of deep compassion for the wandering sheep.

Now there's a little confusion here with the word *wanders*. I don't want to get into a complicated grammar lesson, but in the original language of these verses, it's hard to tell whether James has a person in mind who just wandered off. "Whoa! I'm over here now. I didn't have any plan. I didn't expect to end up in this place. I just woke up one day and wasn't where I used to be." That's one kind of wandering.

But another kind of wandering describes a person who was drawn away, a person who was taken by a wolf. Jesus talked about wolves in sheep's clothing. In Matthew 7:15 He said, **"Beware of false prophets, who come to you in sheep's clothing but inwardly are ravenous wolves."** These lost sheep used to believe the truth, but now they believe error. They used to listen to what was right, but they started listening to what was wrong, and it drew them away. Someone came and got them and took them away.

Both things happen: people foolishly wander off, or negative, destructive relationships come along, get in someone's head, and draw them away. So we have two wanderers in mind: the foolish "how-did-I-get-over-here?" wanderer, and the person who's been led away by someone. Both are true.

Let's pause here for a few moments because the longest journey begins with one step. While the remainder of the chapter focuses on the person who today may be far from the church, we must acknowledge that wandering begins with an initial step.

Kathy and I like to watch some of those news magazine programs. Not long ago we saw a *Dateline* story of a one-year-old Canadian girl named Erika. Somehow she wandered out of her house in the night while her parents were sleeping. She didn't realize where her little steps were taking her and she spent the entire night outside in an Edmonton winter. How cold is that? When her mother found Erika, she appeared to be totally frozen. Her legs were stiff; her body was blue. All signs of life seemed to be gone. But there is a popular saying among rescue workers: No one who's frozen is called *dead*; they're only dead when they're warm and dead. Erika was treated at Edmonton's Stollery Children's Health Center. God helped the doctors bring her back to life. To the amazement of all, there appeared to be no sign of brain damage. They gave her a clear prognosis; she would soon be able to hop and skip and play like other girls her age. Sadly, the outcome of her amazing wanderer story isn't seen often enough in those who wander from the faith.

Maybe as you're reading this chapter, you recognize a warning about your situation. You haven't wandered off yet. You've taken one or two steps in the wrong direction. You're out on the ice right now. You're thinking, "Look at me! I didn't go down! I didn't fall through!"

Listen—take one or two more steps and the ice will shatter. I want you to realize this as we talk about going out and getting the wanderers, *you don't have to be that person.*

You don't have to crash through the ice, devastate your family, and bring that mess to the church in a basket where everyone has to spend months piecing it all back together, because you were too stupid or stubborn to listen. For everyone's sake, we hope you come back sooner rather than later!

You can wake up right now and get back to shore with the rest of us. Stop being foolish and playing around with nonsense that you know is going to trash you and the people you love! Don't do it! Come back! Maybe you've made a foolish decision or allowed desire—a wrong desire—to begin to grow. You're playing with the fire. "See? I'm not singed! I didn't get burned!!" Come back—right now! Receive this word as coming from the

Lord Himself. Don't wander off. Don't think you can beat the odds—you cannot!

"My brothers, if anyone among you wanders from the truth and someone brings him back . . ." Notice, from what do they wander? The Bible answers, *the truth*. This is not a term that invites creative translation—it's straightforward.

Isn't it interesting? It doesn't say, "wanders from Jesus." Now, Jesus *is* the Truth. He said, **"I am . . . the truth."**[5] So in that sense we could say he wandered from Jesus. It doesn't say, "wanders from the church," although the church is implied in the context. The Bible calls it **"the church of the living God, a pillar and buttress of the truth."**[6] Yes, James does include the Lord and the church in this passage. But at the center of it all— the core—is what we believe. God has made some statements and we believe them. When you wander, you are wandering *from* the truth. You're wandering *into* error. How's that going for you, wanderer?

If you're ready to be honest, you would have to say, "Not great."

So it's time to come back. Yes, you come back to a place and to a people; certainly you come back to a Person—God. You will also come back to the truth itself. Jesus said in John 17:17, **"Sanctify them in the truth; your word is truth."** This is very good news because it's a frightening thing to be away from the truth of God's Word. David said in Psalm 119:105, **"Your word is a lamp to my feet and a light to my path."** Think of God's Word as light in your life. People who have wandered from the truth are not in the light; they are in darkness. If you were in a large room that suddenly turned pitch black, you'd be calm for a moment or two. Then someone would scream. And, before long, it could get pretty crazy. It's not great to be in the darkness. **"Your word is a lamp . . . a light to my path."** God's Word is light *and* direction. God's Word shows us where to go, tells us what to do, and helps us know what's right and wrong. It's guidance.

Allow God to begin to stir in your heart what it's like to be in darkness with no sense of direction. Because that's the condition the wanderer finds himself in as he wakes up today. You can pray, "I don't know what he was doing last night. I don't know where he is going this weekend. But if he's out there, he's lost in the darkness. He doesn't know what's up or down. He doesn't know where to go. He doesn't know how to get out. Meet him there, Lord." His condition may seem obvious to the rest of us, but it's not apparent when you're the one in the darkness.

You might say, "It's so clear. They know where they left."

Remember, they lost their way. Wanderers need us to find them! That's what this is all about. We are praying for the same heart Jesus expressed as He looked at the crowds following Him: **"When he saw the crowds, he had compassion for them, because they were harassed and helpless, like sheep without a shepherd."**[7] Jesus left heaven to come find us!

James is inviting our attention: **"If anyone among you wanders from the truth . . ."** Someone has wandered from the truth. Do you have any compassion for this person? Is your

29

heart heavy for them, for the hard situations in which they find themselves?

"You know what? I *told* them this! I warned them. They're just getting exactly what I told them." Is that how you feel? Because that is *so* not God's heart. Just think about what it would be like to wake up today, lost in the darkness. Couldn't God stir compassion in you for such a person?

God loves the wanderer the *same* as He loves you and me. God forgive us for any sort of self-righteous thinking, "They're getting what they deserve." God simply does not respond that way. Not toward them—and not toward us!

Here's the second point. Are you ready for good news?

THE REMEDY IS POSSIBLE.

Complete solutions are not typical in life. Would you agree? A lot of things happen for which there is no remedy.

What do you do at your house when a lightbulb burns out? You don't try to fix it. You change it. That's not really a repair; it's a replacement. You didn't fix the lightbulb. You pitched it and screwed in a new one. What happens to a business that goes bankrupt? You might start a new business, but the current one? You're done with that. You can fix a problem, but you can't fix something that's dead. It's done. It's over.

Now here's the really good news. We could not insist, demand, or require that almighty God receive back wanderers—but He *does*. He welcomes them. He restores them. He forgives. This is crazy—He *celebrates* them! **"There will be more joy in**

heaven over one sinner who repents than over ninety-nine righteous persons."[8] Heaven is fired up every time a wanderer comes home. Isn't that fantastic? So the remedy is possible.

Here in James 5:19 we see it: **"and someone brings him back."** Think of the person you know who's a prodigal—a pleasure-seeking, wounded, ashamed, or distracted wanderer. I want you to begin to picture differently the wanderers you know. Believe God's Spirit is stirring in your heart and bringing to mind a specific person or two for you to approach and attempt to bring back. God is working in all of this. Of course you can think of the obvious person—a son or a daughter or a sister or a brother. The people we love most, the people closest to us, those are the people toward whom our hearts immediately go out.

But let me make a painful observation. Sometimes the obvious wanderer is not the person you'll be able to go get. Chances are you've probably already made a couple of moves in that regard. Reading this might get you all motivated and you will want to get right in their face. "It's time, man! You're coming back right now!" That's not going to go well because you've probably already cashed a lot of chips in their direction. Your wanderer's guard is up. Here's what I'd suggest: God is going to have to touch someone else's heart to go get them. You may come to the place where you realize they'll have to hear it from someone else. So pray for the obvious wanderer, but go get the less obvious one God puts on your heart. Then trust God to put the one closest to you on someone else's heart. I'm not saying you shouldn't do anything, but you may not be the point person

God will use in your loved one's life.

Instead, why don't you think of a person you knew in school or someone you haven't talked to for a long time who would be surprised to hear your voice? You might have to do a little bit of work to even find him or her. Maybe it's a friend you've grown apart from or someone you used to see in church.

A woman in our church wrote a beautiful letter to a couple she used to sit near every week. They would talk. She knew their first names. They would pray together before or after the service. Suddenly, she didn't see them. They were just gone. A few months later she saw the wife in a grocery store. She asked, "What happened to you? Are you okay?" The wife had to hurry, but it was obvious she was really burdened. Something had happened—maybe she was wounded. So our member wrote her a letter. She's trying to get those wanderers. Let God touch your heart with a person like that.

Notice in the text, not just anyone, but . . . "someone." **"If anyone among you wanders from the truth and *someone* brings them back . . ."** *Someone's* got to go get them. God will reach them through a person. Are you anyone's someone?

Actor Kirk Cameron got a lot of attention a few years ago for his work in the movie *Fireproof*. I didn't know him until he invited me to go out to California for an interview on TV. We have since become friends. One of the unusual things about Kirk, which I've kind of teased him about, is that he carries tracts wherever he goes—those little printed gospel presentations—quirky thought provokers. One of the types he hands out is a million dollar bill that has the gospel on the back. Not real money, but a true message.

Kirk is bold with these things. He was at a resort in Santa Barbara and came across a whole bunch of NBA players with their bodyguards. They were sitting around a table having a very private, high-stakes card game. Kirk walked up to the table, pulled out his million-dollar tract, put it down, and said, "I'm in!"

They didn't say a single word to him. They just turned and gave him a look that said, "In? You're going to be in the ground if I'm still looking at you in thirty seconds."

So he said, "Thank you, gentlemen," and backed away from the table, leaving behind his bill.

I'm not trying to put down the tract-leaving approach, but most authentic life change in people I see happens face-to-face and life on life. You won't be able to simply put a "door-knocker invitation" on the wanderer's house and then wait to see them at church. Don't sail a gospel blimp over their neighborhood. It's going to take direct contact and a personal touch.

I was driving down to Indiana this week and saw a huge billboard. In big block letters—white on black—it said, "HELL IS REAL." I seriously doubt a person will be driving down the freeway wandering from God and think, "Wow! Hell is real? Why didn't someone tell me? Okay. That changes *every*thing."

The point is not to cut down the billboard or lose the gospel tract. God bless them—they're trying to do something. The point *is* that God's Word says, **"someone brings him back."** *Someone*. It's a person. Don't just hang a door knocker or hope they drive by a billboard. Don't avoid the tension of a personal contact. Go get the wanderer!

Begin to think, "Who is it for me? Who do I need to go find who didn't immediately leap to mind? Who's not with the Lord right now who I used to love and care for?" They may not know anyone else who can share the hope you have to offer. Meditate on the message of Psalm 126:6, **"He who goes out weeping, bearing the seed for sowing, shall come home with shouts of joy, bringing his sheaves with him."** When we start caring the way Jesus instructs us, we can expect a certain weight of sorrow in the effort. But the joy He promises will make it worthwhile. Go get the wanderer.

THE STAKES ARE HIGH.

Notice how James 5:19–20 continues: **"My brothers, if anyone among you wanders from the truth and someone brings him back, let him know . . ."** There isn't a better word that could have been chosen to give you confidence. *Know* isn't an idea you have to think about. *Know* isn't something you have to wonder about—it is a fact you can bank on. It means *to know as certainty*. **"Let him know, that whoever brings back a sinner . . ."** If **"whoever"** is you, God wants you to know this truth. If you are thinking, "Will I do this? Should I do this?" don't back away. Here's what you need to know. First, the stakes are high in bringing **"back a sinner from his wandering."** The NIV says **"from the error of his way.**[9]**"** Whether it's the sin itself or the wandering the sin has produced, our role remains: **"Whoever**

brings back a sinner from his wandering will save his soul from death." The stakes couldn't be higher. You're going to **"save his soul from *death*.**"

What does *that* mean?

James is not talking about physical death. We know death is coming—for all of us. So obviously, by bringing a wanderer back to the Lord, you're not saving him from physical death. The passage is not talking about the first death, it's talking about the *second* death. As Revelation 20:14–15 says, **"This is the second death, the lake of fire. And if anyone's name was not found written in the book of life, he was thrown into the lake of fire."** It's talking about hell. Bringing back a wanderer is going to save him from hell.

If you're thinking, "I can't save anyone. That's what God does!" You are absolutely right. We're not talking here about people wandering in and out of salvation like some kind of spiritual merry-go-round, where one week you're on and another you're off. One of the characteristics of an authentic Christian is that they continue in the faith. False professions and fake Christians leave and never come back. True Christians, though they may wander, come back.

At this point, if you are following along, you no doubt have a question: "My sister—she's really out there right now. Is she saved?" We don't know. Here's what we *do* know: if she comes back, she was saved. God may have worked through you to bring her back. The fact that she came back is a confirmation that she was saved or, at the very least, is now saved. If she refuses to return, and ultimately dies in that condition, it's confirmation that she never was saved. In any case, it's not for us to decide whether a wanderer needs salvation or restoration—our concern is to go get them!

Philippians 1:6 says, **"And I am sure of this, that he who began a good work in you will bring it to completion at the day of Jesus Christ."** God doesn't give up on any of His children. He is not finished with them until they are finished. He may allow them to wander, but He will not leave them there. We go in His name to bring them back. Their return confirms God's commitment to them.

The stakes are high. If they stay out there, it's an indication they really never knew the Lord and won't be with us in heaven—or they are not yet done wandering.

Because the stakes are so high, finding wanderers is a messy business. You can get your feelings hurt and your toes stepped on. You could get called arrogant: "Who do you think *you* are to tell me anything about my life?" Given these fair warnings, are we selfless enough to risk our own safety and security? God forgive us if we huddle in our holy enclave and don't have our hearts moved for people who are in danger of eternal consequences.

It's a risky business to go after wanderers. You will feel the weight in your heart as you start conceptualizing. Every person who's out there has a little house of cards they built using all their reasons, rationalizations, explanations, and blame-shifting for why they're not in the fold right now. If you talk to them, you're going to hear all that content. Most of them are not waking up today thinking, "Wow! It really stinks out here in Wanderville. I need to go home."

But here's the interesting thing: just let them get in a car accident, or receive a piece of bad news from the doctor. That house of cards will come *crashing* down and they will *call* out to God. In their heart of hearts, they *know* what's true. You have to believe He is at work in their lives.

Even if you are reproved and rebuffed; even if you're put off this time—mark it down—when they start heading back toward the fold, they will remember you as the person who cared enough to go to them even when they didn't want to hear the truth. Go get the wanderer. Show them there's a way back.

James 5:19–20 again says, **"My brothers [and sisters], if anyone among you wanders from the truth and someone brings him back, let him know that whoever brings back a sinner from his wandering will save his soul from death and will cover a multitude of sins."**

The last phrase is the final lesson we can take with us as we look at various wanderers in Scripture. In the rest of this book we will see:

The problem of wandering exists.

The remedy for wanderers is possible.

The stakes are high when we go after wanderers. And last,

THE REWARD IS GREAT.

If you bring back a sinner, you cover a multitude of sins. Psalm 32:1 says, **"Blessed is the one whose transgression**

is forgiven, whose sin is covered." First Peter 4:8 advises, **"Keep loving one another earnestly, since love covers a multitude of sins."** Here is a great truth: you can have a prodigal or a pleasure-seeker out there right now, and when you think about what they might be doing, it can break your heart. But an amazing transformation happens when they come home—when they really come back to you and to the Lord. When a wanderer is restored, we don't spend time talking about *their* sin. It's forgiven!

What did the father of the prodigal do? He waited and waited for that son who was living like a pig. But when he came home, he *ran* to him. He fell upon him and gave him a bone crushing hug! He threw a party for him! That father celebrated with these words: **"Your brother . . . he was lost, and is found."**[10] He came home. Love covers sin.

Here is one of the messages that the wanderer desperately needs to hear. If you're a wanderer, don't miss this. Your past can be forgiven. Your hurts can be healed. Your sin can be atoned for. That's the great truth of the gospel. We celebrate what Jesus Christ has done for sinful people—starting with us! The reward is great.

One of my favorite hymns was written by a man named Robert Robinson. More than a hundred years ago, Robert Robinson composed the great hymn "Come, Thou Fount of Every Blessing." Interestingly, in the second verse, he included the thought, "Prone to wander, Lord I feel it." Do you feel that tendency—your proneness to wander? When we sing that hymn, we ask

God to seal our hearts against that tendency to lose our way.

Curiously, it appears that after Robinson wrote that hymn, *he* walked away from God—not for a year, but for *three decades*. His proneness to wander became a pattern. He tried to get away from it all. Of course, did God go with him? Thirty years after his song was published, Robinson met a young woman who happened to be reading a collection of poetry. He was so distraught that he asked her, "Read to me from your book." She unknowingly read to him the very words of the hymn he had written years before! Imagine the situation. She said, "Oh, listen to this encouraging thought! Someone wrote these words: 'Prone to wander, Lord I feel it. Prone to leave the God I love. Here's my heart, O take and seal it . . .'" Apparently, Robinson not only admitted to having written the lyrics, but also to his deep longing to feel again what he had experienced with God when those words were inspired.

God will go with you as you go get the wanderer. They are often waiting for someone to care. Even if they aren't, we're under orders to make the effort in Christ's name.

God, I pray in this moment that You would, in this reader and myself, stir such a longing, God, such a burden, that we can't escape it. Fill each person reading this with a strong desire to reach those who may be as lost today as they once were. How Your heart longs for these people and how stubbornly we have navigated through life in our own interest or in the interests of those closest to us. But God, I pray You would touch our hearts today with someone we can touch, someone lost in darkness, someone we can go get, Lord. We can speak Your Truth to them. We can reach out to them in love. Let our eyes be not upon the response. Let us focus on obedience. Use us as You see fit.

Lord, I know that we have our own burdens. These are not easy days. Some of us might think, "Going after wanderers is for a different season for me. Right now I need to focus on myself." Lord, cause us to know in our hearts that when we take up the pursuits that matter to You, You rush to our aid. You meet the needs we cannot meet for ourselves. Let us believe that when we have on our hearts what is on Your heart, we are in the best position to receive the things we need.

Cause us to purpose that all we do, we do for Your glory—for Yours alone. In Jesus' name, Amen.

CHAPTER 2

FEARFUL
WANDERER
—COME HOME!

AS WE DISCOVERED in the last chapter, James 5:19–20 supplies us with a compelling invitation to live more attentively when it comes to the wanderers we meet every day: **"My brothers, if anyone among you wanders from the truth and someone brings him back, let him know that whoever brings back a sinner from his wandering will save his soul from death and will cover a multitude of sins."**

"Brings him back" where? The answer is "brings him back home." There's nothing like home. "Home, Sweet Home," we say. What's so sweet about home? Lots of stuff: familiar surroundings, loving support, the people who know you best and keep loving and giving and praying even though they know *everything*. Those are some sweet treasures found at home.

You may ask, "Well, if it's so great, why do people wander

away from their home, away from God? Why do so many people turn away?"

I believe the answer is that many times they don't mean to leave. They just begin following a trail of foul bread crumbs and wake up one day thinking, "What am I doing over here? This isn't what I wanted for my life."

Meanwhile, the invitation goes out each day to come home. Come back to your family. Come back to God.

Some say, "Well my family—that's not so great. I don't get much of an invitation there."

I'm sorry if that's your experience. Just remember that God is your Father, and the church of Jesus Christ can be your family. Come back to what is true. Return to what's right. The invitation to come home isn't just for people who aren't in church; it needs to be heard by those who are in church every week but their heart is not there. People who are not where they're supposed to be and they know it.

PETER, THE WANDERER

Even Peter, one of the disciples, wandered. If someone who shadowed Jesus for three years could get off track and find himself in a bad place, who are we to say that it couldn't happen to us or someone close to us?

In order to recognize the danger of wandering, let's trace Peter's story, starting in Matthew 26. First, a little bit of context. This was now the final week leading up to the crucifixion of Jesus. It began with the triumphal entry and the feeling on the part of the disciples that Jesus' rise to power was about to happen. One evening in Bethany, while they were eating, a woman came in and anointed Jesus by pouring costly perfume on Him. Some of the disciples muttered, "Wow! She should've sold that stuff and given the money to the poor. She wasted an opportunity! She could have helped somebody!"

Jesus said in Matthew 26:12, **"In pouring this ointment on my body, she has done it to prepare me for burial."**

They wondered, "What is He talking about!?" At this point, Matthew notes that Judas went to the chief priests and negotiated his betrayal of Jesus.[1] From then on he waited for the right moment.

Then Passover came and they gathered for the Last Supper in the upper room. Judas' betrayal had been foretold and began to unfold. What fills up five chapters in the gospel of John, Matthew summarizes in ten verses, briefly describing the meal and Jesus' introduction of the Lord's Supper. Then, Matthew 26:30–31 moves on to the rest of the dramatic evening: **"And when they had sung a hymn, they went out to the Mount of Olives. Then Jesus said to them, 'You will all fall away because of me this night.' "** That's a stunningly clear prediction. Who? All of you will . . . what? Fall away. When? It's going to happen *tonight*.

What would have been a good response when Jesus said to Peter and the others, "You're going to fall away from me"? Any one of them could have said, "Lord, I don't want to do that! You know everything, so I have to take this very seriously. But I don't want to fall away. How can we keep this from happening?"

You would think at least *one* of the eleven would have humbled himself (Judas had bailed out by then). But none of them did. In fact, "**Peter answered him, 'Though they all fall away because of you, I will never fall away.'**"[2] Notice the blinding nature of overconfidence. When you are brashly optimistic about something, you are in great danger. Peter was blinded to his own need because he was so impulsively sure of himself.

The word on the street is that I bought a motorcycle not long ago. Some might call it a Hog, but it's more like a horse. People have approached me with worried looks on their faces and asked, "Aren't you known for going too fast?" But here's the truth: I am so scared on this motorcycle that I err on the side of slow. I know if I stop being scared, I will actually put myself in danger. I realize from experience that huge hazards await the overconfident. Scripture says, "**Let anyone who thinks that he stands take heed lest he fall.**"[3] The person who thinks, "I will never wander or struggle. I won't fall. I can handle this," is the person who really is in a very bad way.

Jesus gave Peter another chance. The Lord is so tender here. Peter was trying *so* hard. "I don't care what You say. I'll never fall away." Jesus didn't rebuke him. He wasn't harsh or angry with him; He was firm and clear in Matthew 26:34, "**Jesus said to him, 'Truly, I tell you, this very night, before the rooster crows, you will deny me . . . three times.'**" The Lord was saying, "Not once. Not twice, Peter, but *thrice*. You say *not you*? I say *you* in particular. You say, *never*! I say, *today*!"

Now, does Peter get it? Does he recognize the warning? Does he slap his own forehead and say, "Okay, Lord. Help me! I don't want to do this"?

No, he upped the ante: **"Peter said to him, 'Even if I must die with you, I will not deny you!' And all the disciples said the same"** (v. 35). They were just following Peter's lead—right over the cliff of overconfidence.

That exchange concerns me when I think about how you and I respond to God. Here's Peter, talking *bold*. How wrong is he? Dead wrong. But how right does he *think* he is? Totally right. So he thinks he's standing for Christ, but he's bold in a paper bag. He's completely blind to his own situation. He wants to hold his ground and doesn't see the freight train coming!

In retrospect, he might have sadly said, "He *told* me, but I didn't listen." That's a summary for Matthew 26:30–35.

Peter's experience is the testimony of every wanderer. "She told me, but I didn't listen." "He warned me, but I refused to hear." "They *pleaded* with me, but I sealed my ears." I think it begs this question: Why does the wanderer refuse to listen? Peter was not a foolish person. He wasn't lacking in intelligence in any way. So why does the stubborn person ignore what they are told?

FOUR REASONS WHY THE WANDERER REFUSES TO LISTEN

(1) Immaturity.

They don't know, and they're too slow to grow. They don't realize their condition, so they're not ready to learn yet.

Immaturity is not just people who act silly—in the right setting even mature people can act silly because they don't take themselves too seriously. Immaturity, however, is the *inability to connect actions and consequences.* The immature person is the person who doesn't get it. They don't think, "When I do *this* action, I get *that* reaction or result." They can't make the connection between their choices and what comes because of them. That's immaturity. By the way, this isn't a lesson intended to single out and hammer children and adolescents. Whatever your age, remember this: though you're young just once, you can be immature for life. There are a lot of people who are in their sixties but their maturity hasn't graduated yet from middle school. They just can't see the connection when they ask, "Why does this *always* happen to me?"

They need to discover the unbreakable law of cause and effect that God has established in the universe. You choose to sin; you choose to suffer. That's what's coming. People frequently say, "Well I'm going to beat the odds. I'm going to cut the corners." Then they hit a brick wall or disappear in a bottomless pit. That's one of the reasons why people don't listen—immaturity: too slow to know and to grow.

Here's a second reason people ignore wise warnings. Not immaturity, but . . .

(2) Rebellion.

"My will. My thrill. You chill." Those are the proud declarations of rebellion. "No one's going to get between my will and my thrill! This is what *I* want to do. You back off! Don't tell me anything." They won't listen and they try to cut off any attempts by others to help. They are rebels stuck in overdrive headed for a wall—and they don't care!

Sometimes it's immaturity or rebellion. But sometimes—completely different—it's . . .

(3) Woundedness.

Hidden hurts close hearts and ears. "Why doesn't he listen to me more?" He could be wounded. Something may have happened that left unseen scars. Sometimes in a family, in a church family, things happen that few know about. You hold it all inside and don't deal with it. You're hurting, but you don't bring it out in the open. You're not listening to reason, but it's because you have this hidden wound.

Beyond immaturity, rebellion, or woundedness, sometimes people won't listen because their obstacle is . . .

(4) Relationships.

Peers could be the problem. Peers in the ears block fears. Things we should be afraid of don't register on our radar. I can remember, to my own shame, being about eighteen years old, cruising in my father's 455 horse, four-barrel carburetor Oldsmobile. I was traveling 90 miles per hour, on a country road. Then I hit the gas and felt the engine open up and *vvvrrr-roooom*—I felt the need for speed!

"Were you crazy?"

The answer is *yes*. My actions in that moment were absolutely, insanely foolish.

You ask, "How could you be so stupid?"

Well, there were a lot of reasons for my decisions, but the main one was a friend of mine, over in the passenger seat shouting, "GO!! GO!! GO!!!"

To which you say in your best tone of wisdom, "James! You should have been *terrified*!"

Yes, I should have been scared, but peers in the ears block fears. There are many times we should be afraid, but we're not afraid because we're more concerned about impressing our friends and the people around us. It's a very dangerous place to be, wanderer.

WHEN WE DON'T LISTEN

"He told me," Peter would have to say in regard to the Lord, "but I didn't listen." And it didn't stop there. In Matthew 26:69–75 the wandering went further: "He told me, but I didn't listen, and now I am ashamed by what I've done."

In order to see the steps Peter took in wandering, it helps to pick up the story right after Jesus' arrest in the garden of Gethsemane. Matthew 26:58 tells us Peter was cautiously following the Roman guard and the crowd that were escorting Jesus. Following? He wanted the comfort of knowing what was happening, but he didn't want the association of belonging. So he was tracking from a distance like the wanderer often does. John, who was also following, arranged for Peter to get into the high priest's courtyard, or the big fisherman would have been left out on the street (John 18:15–16).

Matthew 26:69 begins, **"Now Peter was sitting outside in**

the courtyard. [A place where he could hear and maybe see what was going on.] **And a servant girl came up to him and said, 'You also were with Jesus the Galilean.'"**

His response was the equivalent of, "What?!" Verse 70 says, **"But he denied it before them all saying, 'I do not know what you mean.'"**

"You were with Jesus!"

"Me?! Where did you get that idea?" We call that "playing dumb." He was deflecting the obvious truth! Things were getting uncomfortable.

Matthew 26:71–72 continues, "And when he went out to the entrance, another servant girl saw him, and she said to the bystanders, 'This man was with Jesus of Nazareth.' And again he denied it with an oath." Peter used a curse, an expletive, to emphatically say, "I don't know the man!"

"Don't know Him, Peter? Don't know the One who called you? Don't know the One who dubbed you 'the Rock,' who you saw feed five thousand people? He was transfigured before you. You don't *know* Him, Peter?"

"After a little while the bystanders came up and said to Peter . . ." (v. 73). Later, a group of people approached him. When surrounded by wrongdoers, wrongdoing comes easily. The wrong crowd easy leads to the wrong path. So when someone in the crowd said, **"'Certainly you too are one of them, for your accent betrays you.' Then he began to invoke a curse on himself and to swear"** (v. 74). He said something like, "I'd rather burn in hell than be in the company of that guy!"

No one should *ever* make that kind of foolish wish. **"He began to invoke a curse on himself and to swear, 'I do not know the man.' "** Wow! "You were going to die for Him, Peter? Were we a little overconfident earlier? How about some humility?"

"And immediately the rooster crowed. And Peter remembered the saying of Jesus, 'Before the rooster crows, you will deny me three times'" (v. 75). This is one of the saddest phrases in the Bible—**"and he went out and wept bitterly"** (v. 75). Actually, Luke 22:61 tells us that when the rooster crowed, Peter was within view of the Lord, maybe fifty yards away. They made eye contact. Peter saw Jesus right after his third denial, while the crowing echoed in his ears. Then he turned and fled, weeping bitterly. The word translated *bitterly* means *violent, uncontrolled, convulsing sobs*. Head bowed, shoulders heaving. The sobs came in scalding waves of shame and disappointment. Not fake, crocodile tears, but the wordless groans of a broken man. What else could he say but, "I am ashamed by what I've done."

Have you ever been unmasked and shamed like Peter? Hidden in a falsehood one moment, then suddenly exposed the next? Being ashamed, by the way, is not always a bad thing. People say, "You don't ever want to feel shame." Tempting, but incorrect. Even secular people realize that in trying to increase self-esteem, our society has promoted shamelessness without acknowledging the reality that sometimes our behavior *should* make us ashamed. Shame can be a good thing. Even God's prophets in the Old Testament realized shame had a purpose. Jeremiah went on record saying, **"Were they ashamed when**

they had committed abomination? No, they were not . . . they did not know how to blush."[4] When you lose your capacity to feel shame, you are in a very dangerous place.

Here's a good definition. Shame: *the painful feeling arising from a realization that personal actions have brought disgrace.* Shame is the acknowledgment that what I did revealed truth about me and cast a negative light on others as well as on myself. Shame may finally get a wanderer's attention and turn him back toward home.

The problem is, people often have wrong responses to shame. Most of us (make that *all* of us) have done something in our life about which we are totally ashamed. I don't want anyone reading this thinking, "Oh, he's only talking to me. He's isolating me." Shame is a shared human experience. But here is the problem: how do you deal with shame? What do you do with the disgrace? If we never find out, we can live devastated lives.

I appreciate hearing testimonies about the way God deals with shame in our lives. God's grace never leaves us proud of that which brought shame, but it allows us to speak about it in ways that help others.

First, let me show you the wrong way, the way we usually try to deal with shame. Let's let this symbol ● represent the thing I've done that I'm ashamed of. Think about your own shameful example, and whisper or say, "*I've* done it."

Now here are the bad responses. Maybe this is where you live. The first bad response to shame is represented by this shape: ■

Deny my shame. I just block it (■)out. The black circle is hidden behind the black square. "If I can no longer see it behind the cover, it didn't happen." This is what happened to a friend of mine I'll call Anthony. His testimony included the difficult truth that as a child he was taken by someone and abused. When his father found out, he didn't want anyone to know about it. His message to his son was, "You deny the shame. It didn't happen. It's not a problem." But here's the problem you create instead: you bury the shame down inside you, but it's spreading like a cancer in your soul. Denying shame—that's not the way to deal with the shame.

The second way of dealing with the shame was also tried by Anthony and by many of us. We take the

: ● :

And pretend it's shrunk down to

: . :

"I'm going to dilute or minimize the shame. I was abused. Now I'm going to become an abuser. I'm going to pass it on. I hate being alone with these feelings, so I'm going to add others to this circle of shame. I'm just going to perpetuate this in my life." It is shocking how often those who have been abused become abusers in different ways. That is a very, very bad plan for dealing with shame.

Don't deny it.

Don't dilute it and become the abuser yourself.

Another wrong way that people try to deal with shame (I think this is worst of all) is they take their

And they

↓

They despair in their shame. This is what Judas did. Judas said, "I can't take this! I can't be this person. I can't face another day." Satan wants to push us to that extreme. Judas took his life. Anthony told us that he tried to hurt his wife and he tried to hurt himself. These actions make a statement: "I despair of my shame! I can't be this person anymore!" That is an awful, self-destructive way to deal with shame.

The final way—the wrong way—I'm going to picture this way:

People attempt to depart or flee their shame. "Something shameful happened to me when I lived in Elgin. Now I'm going to live in Edinburgh on the other side of the world. I'm going to get as far away as I can from what happened to me. I'm going to leave the people and the place that remind of the pain. I'm going to get away."

Peter began using this last shame tactic as he left the chief priest's courtyard in tears over his shameful performance. His instinctive response is not going to work out great for him. Let's keep chasing down his story in John 21. Peter's experience is a vivid episode we may have to describe to a wanderer as the reason we can say to them, "You don't have to be afraid to come home." We can invite them to see themselves in Peter's place, fearing what Jesus will say.

Peter *was* afraid. He kept replaying in his mind the steps of his wandering.

He told me, but I didn't listen.

I insisted I knew myself better than He did.

I'm ashamed by what I've done.

Now I am afraid to come home.

John 21:1 says, **"After this Jesus revealed himself again to the disciples by the Sea of Tiberias."** There were numerous postresurrection appearances by Jesus Christ, but let's look at what preceded this one. The Sea of Galilee is about sixty miles north of Jerusalem. Peter didn't take a tram up there. That was several days' journey over rough country to get there. Peter's attitude must have been, "Jesus is risen in Jerusalem. That's where I denied the Lord. He probably doesn't want me around." So he walked with some other disciples up to the north side of the Sea of Galilee.

John 21:3 is a flashback to set the scene: **"Simon Peter said to them, 'I am going fishing.'"** In other words, that's a big step backward from being fishers of men to being fishermen again. Peter thought Jesus was the source of his shame, so he made the awful decision to get as far away from the Lord as he possibly could. Why was he running? Because of his shame.

What should he have done?

REPENTANCE SHATTERS SHAME

Don't miss this: repentance shatters shame. Peter should have fallen to his knees. He should've said, "I'm wrong! I'm wrong!

I'm wrong! I've been wrong since day one. It's all my fault. I have no one to blame but myself!" He should've leaned into the grace and forgiveness of the Lord. He should have run to His arms and found the forgiveness and cleansing he so desperately needed.

Peter is our example of how *not to do shame*. You don't have to live in your sin. You don't have to wallow in the mire of your failure. You can be washed! You can be cleansed! You can be forgiven! You can have a fresh start. You can have your whole life turned around. That's a big part of what we celebrate and sing about every time we gather to worship. Glory to God! He frees us from our shame.

Grace was right there for Peter, but he wouldn't embrace it. He ran from it. He thought Jesus was the problem, when He was the Solution. So he said, "I am going fishing." How sad. How painful. He could have shattered his shame with repentance, but he supersized it by running and hiding. He was afraid to come home.

So there's Peter—as far away as he can get—filled with shame, floating on a dark sea. John 21:3 records how quickly he returned to an old, familiar pattern: **"They went out and got into the boat, but that night they caught nothing."** Don't you think that's an awesome miracle? They didn't catch *anything*. That's a miracle. These guys were fishermen. They knew the hot spots on the lake. They knew how to cast the nets. This wasn't fishing with a pole and lure, casting all night without a bite. They were throwing big nets weighted with rocks out across the water and pulling them in! When the Bible says they caught nothing, it means the nets were empty every time! They didn't see a single tuna, tilapia, tiny mackerel, minnow, or starfish. Nada! It's a miracle!

That's what God always does when we're wandering. He speaks into our frustrations. "Coming up empty again? It's not working out so great for you? It's not what you'd thought it would be?" Hear His whisper, humble yourself, and come home! Humble yourself and return running to the One who loves you, will forgive you, and will wash your heart clean.

You say with Peter, "Well, I'm afraid to come home." Let me tell you this: your fear is irrational. If you examine it, that fear won't make sense. Fear is a false barrier holding you back.

I have some irrational fears. I was out with my parents at Giordano's the other night. The pizza wasn't quite right. So the waiter came over and said, "I'll take it back to the kitchen."

I said, "NO! No!!! We're not taking that option." Don't ever send your food back to the kitchen, ever! Here are words to live by: do *not* send your food back to the kitchen. You do not know what's going on back there!

Then the manager came over with a fork in hand. He said, "Let me just check—"

"Don't touch it! Put down the fork and step away from the pizza. It's FINE! We will live with it!"

You would probably say, "James, you were a little worked up about that situation."

You're right; that response was irrational. Didn't I just tell you that? It's not rational. Just like the fear that drives the wanderer is not rational.

A wanderer thinks, "If I go home, I'm going to get an earful. I will come back to the Lord and back to church, but *everyone's* going to look down their nose at me. They are going to make me feel awful and filthy."

You are so wrong! That is an *irrational* fear. It's not the way it really is. We *love* you. We've been praying for you. We've been waiting for you. And *God* has been waiting for you. The Bible says, **"There will more joy in heaven over one sinner who repents"**[5] than over a bunch of people who don't think they need it. Your return is the moment we're all waiting for—for you to figure it out like *we* had to figure it out!

So, what's the best reason to realize our fears are irrational? Because we're coming home to Jesus. Let's look at how He handled Peter the wanderer starting in John 21:4: **"Just as day was breaking, Jesus stood on the shore."** I am tremendously comforted by the presence of Jesus on the shore of any place in my life!

JESUS CHRIST'S RESPONSE TO THE FEARFUL WANDERER
• **He lovingly pursues the wanderer.**

Jesus didn't stay down in Jerusalem. He went the sixty miles north and He got to where they were. He lovingly pursues the wanderer. Let me ask you several questions: Has Jesus Christ been pursuing you? Do you strive to avoid truth and truthtellers through whom His Spirit can speak to you? Do you fear downtime and alone time when His Spirit can corner you and really talk to you about where you are? Do you secretly long for peace but fear the journey to a better place? Do you find in your spirit right now that you're squirming because you know you're not where you've wanted to be? Let the Lord speak to your heart today and hear the message that the fearful wanderer can come home. He lovingly pursues you.

This next episode with Jesus has meant so much to me. We can visualize how He stood on the shore and waited all night until the time was right. He shouted in the morning light, "You guys haven't caught any fish, have you?" If you read this question with a tone of reproof you've missed the spirit of Jesus. He must have been smiling in anticipation of what He was about to do *for* them and *to* them! He asked them, **"Children, do you have any fish?"** (v. 5).

To which they answered in unison, **"No!"** (v. 5). They didn't recognize Him yet, and their response meant, "Duh. Would we still be out here if we had had any luck?"

Moments later they cast on the other side of the boat and got an enormous, miraculous catch. They rushed to shore, hoping the nets wouldn't rip. In his haste, Peter put on his clothes and jumped in the water (a very Peter thing to do) when he recognized it was the Lord—the best decision he had made in a long time. Then they counted the fish and cleaned a few for breakfast. Jesus broke the bread and gave it to them in verse 13. Just like old times again, on the road with Jesus.

Notice John 21:15, **"When they had finished breakfast, Jesus said to Simon Peter . . ."**

• Jesus patiently waits to speak.

I wish I had understood the value of patience earlier in my life. I've always been the person who thinks, "I'm going to say it now. It needs to be said. I'm going to say it immediately." I have to acknowledge Jesus wasn't hurried or impatient. I see Him picking His time.

Days earlier, in John 20:19, we find Jesus' first appearance to His disciples after the resurrection: **"On the evening of that day, the first day of the week, the doors being locked where the disciples were for fear of the Jews, Jesus came and stood among them."** Jesus could have immediately confronted the elephant in the room. We wouldn't be surprised if He had said, "Before we get into anything, Peter, we need to talk. Here's a hint: Cock-a-doodle-doo! Could've *died* for Me, huh? What's up now!?" Jesus did nothing like that with Peter.

You may have had a lame pastor or a weak parent who treated you that way, but that's not the Lord. I studied the sequence of events here carefully. Six times Jesus had a chance to challenge Peter—but He never spoke about their "situation" until the sixth time. And when He did speak to him, He waited all night while they were fishing and catching nothing, waited while they came to shore, waited through the whole breakfast as He served them. He waited for the right time to talk to Peter.

• Jesus calls for a clear decision.

John 21:15 continues, **"When they had finished breakfast, Jesus said to Simon Peter, 'Simon, son of John, do you** love me more than these?'"

"More than these what?"

"More than these fish and the life they represent?" They had counted them (v.11). There were 153 fish in the net. That was his old life. That wasn't the person he was supposed to be any more. He pulled Peter aside for a crucial question because the time was exactly right.

Jesus lovingly pursues the wanderer, patiently waits to speak, and He calls for a decision. "Peter?" Not a big speech or a lecture. Not a rehearsing of the past. Just this: "Peter, do you love Me more than these, this life that I've called you from, this thing that really was never so great for you, even this shame you're carrying? Do you love Me more than this?"

Notice that He calls him "Simon, son of John." His nickname was Peter; Jesus always called him Peter—that's the name He gave him. But this moment was more serious than a nickname. It's like with our kids, right? When I call my first son Luke James MacDonald, he knows it's time for a serious talk. This isn't going to be nice chat—not when you roll out the names. "Do you know who you are, Simon? I know who you are. I know your family. I know it *all*. It's time to get back to your identity, Peter—who you really are." I love the way Jesus has done that for me, and I know He will do it for you.

Jesus not only calls for a clear decision, He goes beyond.

• **Jesus assures that purpose is possible.**

After Jesus asked, "Do you love Me more than these?" Peter said in John 21:15, **"Yes, Lord; you know that I love you."**

Peter was expressing the caution learned from failure. Weeks before he would have blurted, "Absolutely, Lord. You can count on me." Now he was hoping Jesus would find his faith true.

"He said to him, 'Feed my lambs'" (v. 15).

"What, Jesus?! I denied You three times. How can You trust me with *anything*?"

"It's all right, Peter. You did it. You blew it. But I'm not done with you yet." Jesus didn't even have to review the past, because it was over. He wanted Peter to know, "I'm not done with you yet! Yeah—you failed! Yeah, you've fallen. But in My plans, you're *still* going to be used."

Now that's grace. "Get up! Come home, Peter. There's a place for you. You're going to be used."

"Really, Lord? I still get to feed Your sheep? It's not over for me?"

When Jesus shows up, He assures us that purpose in our lives is possible. That's a good word for you today. Receive that hopeful message—it's God speaking to you. He's not done with you yet. It's not too late for you, wanderer.

Notice though . . .

• **Jesus insists on true commitment.**

Not once but three times in John 21:15–17 Jesus asked him, "Peter, do you love Me?" "Peter, do you love Me?" "Peter, do you love Me?"

Each time, Peter had to answer, "Yes, Lord. I love You." "Yes, Lord, You know that I love You." "Yes, Lord, You know all things so You've got to know that I love You." The exchange was awkward, but it was necessary.

So why did Jesus ask three times? Something else happened three times just a couple of weeks earlier. Can you remember what it was? How many times did Peter deny the Lord? Three times. So we're going to have three points of clarification—not one question—calling for a true commitment and restoration. "Do you love Me?" "Do you love Me?" "Do you love Me? Here's your chance!"

Peter's answers point the way for every wanderer. "Lord, I can't deny it. I do love You. It's what I really want. I didn't want to stay where I wandered away. I was too prideful. I was too self-confident. Now I know how wrong I was."

Jesus not only welcomes Peter home, but

• He refuses to sugarcoat reality.

"This is going to be hard, Peter. If you're going to follow Me, the way won't be easy. Feeding My sheep is going to take everything you've got." John 21:18 records Jesus' sobering words. "'Truly, truly, I say to you, when you were young, you used to dress yourself and walk wherever you wanted, but when you are old, you will stretch out your hands, and another will dress you and carry you." What did He mean by, "where you do not want to go"? We know what Jesus meant because of John's side note in verse 19: **"(This he said to show by what kind of death he was to glorify God.)"** Church history records that in about AD 65 Peter was executed in Rome under orders from Nero. He had a great life of serving God, but he had a tough finish.

Following Christ is not easy. It's just best. We're not sugar-coating anything here. The Christian life is not always smooth going, but it is exactly what we were designed to do and be. It's the real life. It's the best life you can possibly have: giving your life to Jesus Christ; living for Him; obeying His Word; fellow-shipping with His people; serving in His kingdom. Come home to that life!

And lastly,

• Jesus keeps the focus simple.

At the end of that conversation with Peter, Jesus wrapped it up with, **"Follow Me."**

"What do you want from me?" Isn't that the question you want to ask Jesus?

"I just want you to follow Me. Just do what I say. 'Follow Me' is what I said when I first called you (Matthew 4:19), and it's what I still want you to do. Don't lose sight of Me again and you'll have a great life. Follow Me." That's the reception you will get from Jesus. That's what the fearful wanderer needs—to come home.

We watch *American Idol* at our house. We've got a lot of singers in our family and friends circle. The fourth season introduced us all to Carrie Underwood. Wow! Her hit song "Jesus, Take the Wheel" captures in today's language the surrender Peter had to experience in coming home.

The song is about a woman who is driving on an icy road and loses control, but the car part is really a metaphor for life.

Things were out of control. She was going in a direction she didn't want to go, heading to a place she didn't want to be. Her prayer was, "Jesus, take the wheel. Take control. I'm making a mess of things. It's not what I want for my life."

If you're reading this and realize you're the wanderer who has been fearful to come home, I want to assure you there is a loving, safe place with God's children in the presence of Christ. There you can humble yourself as we all have had to do. Confess those areas and ways in which you have failed the Lord, and receive His forgiveness. Start now—come home.

More than a hundred years ago, D. L. Moody was on his deathbed. A man came to visit him—he just had moments left. The man's name was William Thompson. D. L. Moody said an amazing thing to his visitor, "I would rather have written the words to your hymn than anything I've been able to do my whole life." Moody was referring to a song of invitation Thompson penned called "Softly and Tenderly." The haunting lyrics describe so well what Jesus does, "Softly and tenderly, Jesus is calling, calling for you and for me." And the call on Jesus' heart is the same for each of us: "Come home. You who are weary, come home."

I want to invite you—if God is stirring in your heart the desire to humble yourself—don't wait. Be the wanderer who returns. What a great place to shed some tears, loved one, sitting with an open book and God's Spirit speaking to your heart. No one's judging you. No one who matters is thinking anything but praying you will find the grace of God that we have found. He is "a God merciful and gracious . . ." Compassionate. ". . . Slow to anger, abounding in steadfast love," the Scripture says.[6] There's no good reason for you to delay in coming home.

CHAPTER 3

DOUBTFUL
WANDERER
—COME HOME!

JAMES 5:19–20 provides each of us who are followers of Jesus with a grand mission and a reason to take it on:

> My brothers, if anyone among you wanders from the truth and someone brings him back, let him know that whoever brings back a sinner from his wandering will save his soul from death and will cover a multitude of sins.

We are discovering that while wandering is a problem in the church, the reasons that cause people to drift away are different in each case. In this chapter, we want to talk about the doubting wanderer. Doubts can provoke the wandering or they can keep the wanderer from coming home. In either case, the doubts have to be settled. Maybe that word *doubtful* in the title struck an immediate chord in you. "That's me, I can't move because I doubt. I'm stuck. How do I get past these nagging uncertainties? Can they really be settled?"

John 20 includes the story of one of Jesus' disciples who, after the resurrection, had a hard time believing his fellow disciples had seen the Lord alive. He was hampered by doubts. It might interest you to see how Jesus dealt with him. But first, let's read what happened.

> Now Thomas, one of the Twelve, called the Twin, was not with them when Jesus came. So the other disciples told him, "We have seen the Lord." But he said to them, "Unless I see in his hands the mark of the nails, and place my finger into the mark of the nails, and place my hand into his side, I will never believe." Eight days later, his disciples were inside again, and Thomas was with them. Although the doors were locked, Jesus came and stood among them and said, "Peace be with you." Then he said to Thomas, "Put your finger here, and see my hands; and put out your hand, and place it in my side. Do not disbelieve, but believe." Thomas answered him, "My Lord and my God!" Jesus said to him, "Have you believed because you have seen me? Blessed are those who have not seen and yet have believed."[1]

Using Thomas as our guide let's look more closely at doubters. It's not difficult to anticipate doubt, but it often gets overlooked. Where I hang out we don't talk about doubt a lot;

church is a place of faith. People assume church is a doubt-free zone. And sometimes people find it very hard to admit at church that they sometimes have doubts. But it's really easy for your mind to be filled with uncertainty. We may hide our doubts from others, but the longer they remain unsettled, the more likely we are to wander.

DOUBTING IN THE DARK

Kathy and I—long before we launched Harvest Bible Chapel—were active in children's ministry. I was a youth pastor. One of the things we used to love to do with our high school students was to take them on a summer trip to Algonquin Park in northern Ontario. We would transport canoes out into the wilderness—as far as sixty miles from any road. We couldn't take any cans, bottles, or other potential polluting objects into the backcountry. The trip involved primitive camping and portaging between lakes—a real adventure for many young people.

One night in particular, Kathy and I were asleep in our tent between the girls' camp on one side and the guys' camp on the other. We were awakened by an unusual noise—something was moving around outside our tent. There are many wild animals in the wilderness, but now one was in our camp! I thought for a moment—yes, we had remembered to raise all of our provisions in bags up in a tree so a bear (or other animal—we were more concerned about the bears) couldn't come and get them. That meant the only edible things in camp were us!

I remember lying in my sleeping bag, listening to the

creature rooting around outside with only a thin wall of nylon between us. The noise was big and loud. I can't think of another time when I was more scared in my life. I knew that bears don't come in packs, but I pictured a pack of grizzlies out there, scarring the trees and the ground, sharpening their claws to work on me. But since I was the big protector of all the students, I had to venture forth, armed with my flashlight. I was trembling as I unzipped the tent and poked my head out . . . only to see several little raccoons scurry into the darkness! How could such small creatures make such terrifying noise? Until my eyes corrected what I was hearing, I was filled with fear and doubt.

My point isn't to illustrate the highlights of my adventurous side. I want to show that, like me in that tent in the middle of nowhere, when you're in the darkness, doubting comes easily. Isolation and blindness heighten doubts and fears. You can get your mind so off track and in such a bad place when you can't see. That's why we must keep God's Word in our hands. It is the light shining brightly on the subject of doubt.

Keep in mind that our goal right now is to analyze the condition of doubting among wanderers—not to resolve all doubts with rational arguments. That would be another book.

KINDS OF DOUBTERS

All doubting is not created equal. Doubt has different triggers in people's lives. If you are going to get the doubting wanderer, it's worth understanding what fuels their doubts.

The Empirical Doubter

The empirical doubter is the scholar, student, or intellectual who says in effect, "Believing would require information that I don't have. I've got questions. I have issues. I see problems. I need more information or I won't be able to believe in God, in His Word, or in the gospel."

We wonder, "What information do they need?" Empirical doubters are not a modern phenomenon. Some of them are honest; some are not. Both kinds show up in the Bible. When Pilate asked Jesus, "What is truth?"[2] he was playing the role of an empirical doubter. When a recently healed blind man told Jesus, "And who is he [the Son of Man], sir, that I may believe in him?"[3] he was expressing his willingness to believe, but "I need a little more information!"

Because we can't always tell when a doubter's response is honest and when it is avoiding the need for faith, here are some areas where we must be prepared to give an answer when a doubter raises questions as an explanation for his or her uncertainty. Each of these can be answered reasonably for an honest doubter.

Five Areas of Difficulty for the Empirical Doubter

• **Evidence for the existence of God.**

Empirical doubters will often say, "I'm not even sure if there really *is* a God. How do I know if there's a God?"

In the most basic philosophical thought, you really have just two choices in settling that question: either you believe that there's an unknown (or perhaps knowable) cause of the universe called God; or you believe that all that we see came from no cause at all. Now this is where Norman Geisler's excellent book *I Don't Have Enough Faith to Be an Atheist*[4] can be a resource. He makes the case that it takes a lot more faith to believe that the complexity of the human eye, for example, came from nothing, really—no cause, no force, no design—just one fortunate but completely accidental development in a mind-boggling universe of random but strangely organized systems that simply sprang into existence. Really? It's very hard for me to believe that intricate design doesn't at least hint at a Designer!

Take, for example, Mount Rushmore, the amazing rock formation in South Dakota. When you stand in a certain place below the mountain, you suddenly realize that the cliffs bear an uncanny resemblance to the faces of four American presidents. Then you remind yourself those shapes were purely an odd result of wind, rain, and time, with maybe some lightning and an earthquake or two involved, and voilà, Jefferson, Washington, Lincoln, and Roosevelt! Until one day people noticed and said, "Check it out! The stone presidents! Let's declare this a national park!" But imagine a thousand years from today if we forgot that people actually carved those figures with chisels, hammers, drills, and explosives, and someone suggested, "We don't know how those faces got there, but it just took a lot of time. No one designed that—it was an accident of the elements." Really?

Consider how incredibly simple a sculpture in the side of a mountain is compared to, say, the original functioning human heads it actually represents? Of course, neither those presidents nor their images came from nothing! Both the versions in the flesh and in stone had designers and artists. You can study much more complex and sophisticated rationales for the existence of God in books like the one by Dr. Geisler I mentioned above.

- **Evidence for creation versus evolution.**

Probably the greatest single act of villainy in modern scholarship is the perpetuation of evolution taught as fact when it is only theory. The offense can be found everywhere in the educational system. So much could be said about the real problems with the theory. But just the gaps in the fossil records by themselves, to me, almost negate the theory of evolution.

Textbooks are full of impressive artistic renderings showing how reptiles came from fish and birds came from reptiles, but the illustrations are from imagination rather than the fossil record. And how did all that gradual change happen again?

"It took a lot of time—millions of years!"

So why, in the fossil record, don't we see any transitional forms? How come we don't find the half-fish/half-reptile and the many other mixes that would be necessary for the process to actually happen? Where's that wild assortment in the fossil record? Why don't we see the reptile that was *almost* a bird? We've been digging around for a long time. The absence of transitional life-forms—by itself—almost negates the explanation that it all came together through a process over mind-numbing stretches of time.

To which you might respond with the empirical doubter, "Intelligent design is also just a theory."

I agree—it's a theory that I believe is based on evidence. I didn't check my mind at the door. As I examine and question the evidence, there are rational reasons for believing that design came from a Designer.

• **Evidence for miracles.**

Science is famous for claiming there *cannot* be miracles, yet scientific doctrine also asserts this point: *Anything not repeatedly observable is not true. Empirical certainty is attained by the proof of repetition.* That's a huge thing in scientific theory. If it doesn't happen as a course of regularity, according to natural law, it's not believable. If it doesn't happen repeatedly, observably—it's not true.

So how often did the Big Bang happen?

"Oh, that's an exception. That just happened one time."

And how many people saw it?

"No one saw it."

Not true then! Let's all live by our own rules here, can we, please? Where did life come from?

"Well there was this primordial ooze and it came together with maybe some lightning—we're not sure. And *ZAP!* There was the first living thing; it came from deadness."

Okay, um . . . and how often has that happened since?

"No, it just happened that one time."

Who was present to observe and record the event?

"Well, of course, nobody could be there to see it. There were no people."

Yeah, but you claim "anything that is not repeatedly observable is not true." So which is it?

It's nonsense. Of course, if there's a God, there are miracles. God, by definition, is Someone who can do onetime things anytime He wants, whether anyone else is watching or not!

• Evidence for the resurrection of Jesus Christ.

As often as I've studied the Scripture record of the resurrection myself, I am profoundly touched by it. The evidence, both internal as well as external to the Bible, for the truth of Jesus' resurrection is stunning. Almost every generation has produced fresh efforts by doubters and skeptics to produce the exposé of the real reason for the empty tomb, but who have themselves come to the humbling realization of the truth of Jesus' claims and actions. Men like Frank Morrison (*Who Moved the Stone?*), C. S. Lewis (*Mere Christianity* and *Miracles*), Lee Strobel (*The Case for Christ*), and many others have taken a run at disproving the resurrection and ended up as followers of the risen Lord.

• Evidence for the reliability and the miraculous nature of the Bible.

Why do I believe the Bible? I'm not going to go into those matters at great length here except to say there are rational reasons why I believe the Bible—both internal and external to the Bible; things that have nothing to do with what the Bible says. This has been such a passion for me that I authored *God*

Wrote a Book[5], in which I reference a number of resources that have been helpful for students and doubters. Every person who is a follower of Jesus should have in their hands, in their hearts, and in their minds the evidence for the reliability of Scripture.

Answering the Empirical Doubter

The empirical doubter claims lack of information as a barrier to belief. But let me ask: is it information you don't *have* or information you don't *want*? The truths of Christianity have satisfied the greatest minds in human history. Most of us are not even capable of framing a question for which there is not an *excellent*, satisfying answer in Scripture. Yet people hold God at a distance through a pseudo-intellectualism that perpetuates doubt rather than choosing to search it out and investigate. If you have real questions, there are good answers. Christianity's skin is not so thin that an honest skeptic needs to be fearful of asking the wrong questions. Present your questions and get good answers. Here are some authors you should be reading:

- Norman Geisler, a great Christian apologist. I have already mentioned his book *I Don't Have Enough Faith to be an Atheist*. He is a brilliant scholar. If you are struggling with doubts—intellectual doubts—get answers.
- Phillip Johnson, who wrote the books *Darwin on Trial* and more recently (2004) *The Right Questions*. He's considered the "father of the intelligent design movement," a controversial figure, but a brilliant scholar.
- William Craig's books *Reasonable Faith* and *A Reasonable*

Response. He is a brilliant man, yet in a world that scoffs at the possibility of deep-thinking faith, the truths of Christianity completely and totally satisfy his intellect. And they will yours, too, if you seek out answers.

- Lee Strobel writes, I think, wonderfully and popularly in his books *The Case for Christ*, *The Case for the Creator*, and *The Case for Faith*. These are helpful books for wanderers.

If you are an intellectual doubter, you have to ask yourself the question: is it that I don't *have* the answers or is it that I don't *want* the answers? Because the answers are available—and they will satisfy that good mind that God has given to you.

Here's a second kind of doubter. We'll call him the

The Disillusioned Doubter

This doubter says, "Believing would require conclusions I don't see. I just can't make God work with what's around me." Many have struggled with apparent paradoxes. "If God is real, why is the world so messed up? If God is in charge, why does suffering, murder, rape, and evil saturate society? If God cares, why are famine, disease, and natural disaster rampant around the globe?" This is how the problem of evil is settled in my mind. When the question "If God is good, why is there suffering in the world?" is asked, we must first consider our understanding of omnipotence.

Yes—God is omnipotent—which means *all-powerful*.

Yes—God can do anything.

Except—as I always say when we get to this part—*God can't*

do things that can't be done. For example, God can't lie, the Bible says (Titus 1;2; Hebrews 6:18).

"He could lie if He really wanted to."

No, He cannot! God cannot lie. It's not in His nature to do it. He's a God of truth and without iniquity.

"But God is awesome. He can do anything!"

No, He cannot. He cannot do absolutely anything. He can't make a round square or a married bachelor. If you're married, you're married. God can't do things that can't be done.

Some people used to debate: "Can God make a rock so big He can't lift it?" No, He cannot. Because no matter how big He made it, He could still lift it. There are some things God can't do. He certainly won't do anything that violates His character!

Now think with me about the kind of world God decided to make. He wanted a place where people were free to choose. You may say, "I wish He hadn't made a world like this one," but you're not in charge. God wanted to create people who were able to make choices.

I've heard people suggest, "Why doesn't God just show us who He is in all His majesty and then we would all fall on our faces and worship Him!" But that would not be worship; it would be coercion. This is a key sentence: *God prefers the sincere worship of those who choose Him, rather than the robotic worship of the masses.*

Trust me on this: God could show up in your bedroom tonight and you'd be worshiping before your face hit the floor. But God doesn't want forced adoration. Instead, He has put His fingerprints everywhere. God has given us all the signals. The worst detective in the world can follow the clues: There's a God. **"The heavens declare the glory of God, and the sky above proclaims his handiwork."**[6] God has put eternity **"into man's heart,"**[7] the Scripture says. He has promised, **"If you seek him, he will be found by you."**[8] God wants to be found. He wants to be known. God wants to be believed in and trusted. He appeals to us in many compelling ways, but He will not coerce us. He's given us a choice.

Question: Could God make a world in which people are free to choose—truly free to decide—and, at the same time, guarantee that everyone would choose Him?

Answer: No, He could not. All of the pain, all of the heartache, and all of the suffering in this world are the result of people not choosing God. The original sin of man, confirmed by every person in every generation since, has left the world in shambles. But, like our first ancestors, we desperately want to find someone else to blame for what our choices produce.

At this point skeptics will often ask, "What about natural disasters? Whose fault are they? What's the point in calling them "acts of God" if we can't blame Him when they happen?"

Isn't it interesting how adamant people can be about blaming God for anything they see as bad, while refusing to give Him credit for the fire hose of blessings that He allows in their lives? A thousand idyllic sunsets on the beach are taken for granted, but a tsunami instantly provokes the wrath of man against God. After a devastating mix of natural, personal, and direct human disasters, Job asked a question we need to ask more often: **"Shall we receive good from God, and shall we not receive evil?"**[9] Job realized that living in a fallen world means experiencing just how messed up creation is because of sin. **"The whole creation has been groaning together in the pains of childbirth,"** Romans 8:22 says. The world is broken because of sin. This whole thing is winding down in a hurry. Jesus pointed out that God sends **"the rain on the just and the unjust."**[10] The Bible says that even the goodness of God **"should** (lead to) **repentance."**[11]

Just the fact that you get life, breath, and another day in this beautiful universe, as well as a chance to choose the One who made you, should soften your heart toward Him. He is calling out to you in every moment of every day, "I'm here! I'm real! I love you." He reached out in His Son, Jesus Christ, and provided the payment for our sins so that we could be reconciled to a holy God. Why aren't we overwhelmed by *those* acts of God?

He's done all the real work! All you have to do is realize, "For real. He did it, I need it," and be saved from your sin and wandering. You know you have met God when you can't wait to say, "I need His forgiveness. I believe in Him." The turning point in the gospel is, **"Believe in the Lord Jesus Christ, and you will be saved."**[12] He's just asking for a little step of faith, and then He will rush upon your life with transformation. He will cause the Word of God to come alive to you. He will put His Spirit within you and begin to grow and change your heart and life. God will do so much if you surrender our disillusions.

The Disappointed Doubter

Many people are deeply distressed to discover we must come to God on His terms, not ours. Disappointed doubters often admit that believing would require forgiveness they don't desire to give. "In order for me to believe in God, I'm going to have to settle some things that I don't want to settle." This is the person who is bitter. Something deeply hurtful happened to them and now they are angry, desiring revenge—payback. If you are a disappointed doubter, you want to see someone suffer the way they made you suffer. Until that happens, you don't think you've got time for God.

Here's how God gets in the middle of our hunger for fairness: "In order for me to embrace God with my whole heart, I've got to come to grips with the fact that He allowed something awful to happen in my life. I've got to forgive that person. I've got to embrace God's will for me as having a good purpose even though I can't see it or imagine it." Unsettled offenses keep a lot of people away from God. They want God, but they also want to keep their anger, though they know it's not possible. Do you know any disappointed doubters?

Doubt fueled by angry disappointment has probably been—as I think back over twenty years—the hardest thing for me in my faith. I think of times where we felt attacked or betrayed by people we have embraced and elevated. How do you let that go, move forward, and keep being faithful when you get so disillusioned with people? It's very hard not to revel in someone's misfortune when that person has caused us pain. It goes against our nature to rejoice when God blesses them. We have to remember what Jesus said in the Sermon on the Mount about the blessings wrapped in persecution and hardship.[13] Paul made that insight the basis for a command in Romans 12:14, **"Bless those who persecute you."** Jesus set the bar high for us when He said, **"Love your enemies . . . pray for those who spitefully use you and persecute you."**[14] Forgiveness is the thing that displaces the spiritual barrier in the disappointed doubter.

Here is a definition we find it helpful to repeat often: Forgiveness is the decision to release a person from the obligation that resulted when he or she injured you. I'm working on a very big forgiveness right now. And I'm not there yet. But here's what I know: If I don't get there, my faith will just start to go down, down, down, down, down, down, down. That's how people wipe out and start wandering. I know what God wants me to do and I'm working on it. I'm not there yet, but every day I'm on it.

Sometimes, the reason people sink into doubt is because believing would require forgiveness we don't desire enough ourselves to give to someone else. The huge lesson from Jesus' parable of the unforgiving servant[15] is that we can't have forgiveness if we are not willing to pass it on to others. Do you want to keep gripping that hot coal of unforgiveness ever more tightly as it burns into you? Don't you want to let it go? Haven't you learned, as I've had to learn, that you absolutely must let it go and forgive, that you might experience deeper forgiveness yourself?

You may think, "But you don't know what they did to me."

No, I don't, but God knows, and says you must forgive.

Sometimes I revel in Paul's assurance: " . . . **since indeed God considers it just to repay with affliction those who afflict you.**"[16] Amen! If something needs to be made right, God can handle it; I can't. "Take care of it, God!" The disappointed doubter's pathway home comes through forgiveness—their own and others.

And lastly—I think this next one is the most common cause for doubts that block faith.

The Moral Doubter

The moral doubter makes his case in the following manner: "In order to embrace God by faith with my whole heart, I'd have to make some changes I frankly don't want to make." Instead, the moral doubter perpetuates the condition of uncertainty to avoid the implications of a Supreme Being. Among these are:

- If God is supreme, then I am not a free moral agent.
- If God is supreme, then I must live as my Creator requires.
- If God is supreme, then I cannot do what I want with impunity.

Romans 1:18 tells us that moral doubters **"suppress the truth in unrighteousness."**[17] They know what they are doing, but they don't appreciate what it is costing them—peace with God now and an eternity with Him later.

Do you remember those little jack-in-the-boxes we used to have when we were kids? Spin the handle, hear the familiar tune, "All around the mulberry bush, the monkey chased the weasel" then you brace yourself for the flap to spring and, "Pop goes the weasel!" I think God is like that in many people's lives. As the music of life plays out, POP! God shows up. Push down the flap—there, God is gone. Maybe He was just your imagination. The music goes on—POP! And there God is again! The problem with willfully doubting God's appearances is that you are really revealing an attitude: "I don't want to *answer* to Him. I don't want to *explain* what I'm doing." But you can't get away from Him. In one way or another, He will continue to show up.

David wondered, **"Where shall I go from your Spirit? Or where shall I flee from your presence?"**[17] He had to admit there was nowhere to escape God. Psalm 23:6 talks about God's pursuit: **"Surely goodness and mercy shall follow me all the days of my life."** Haven't you seen the persistence of the goodness and mercy of God? Francis Thompson called God's pursuit the hound of heaven because He never gives up. Every day I throw my feet over the side of the bed and there's the goodness and the mercy of God—so undeserved; so completely unmerited—wooing my heart.

Doubter of every kind, let doubt go instead of holding on to it as if it can explain your life or give you direction. Find in the Lord all that you've been longing for. He's been pursuing you every step of your wandering.

HOW GOD DEALS WITH DOUBTERS

When we want to find out what God does with doubters, we can start with the world's most famous doubter. His name is used frequently when someone expresses uncertainty: "You're just a Doubting Thomas!"

John 20:24 begins, **"Now Thomas, one of the Twelve, called the Twin."** The Greek for *twin* is *Didymus*. We don't know who his twin was. Sometimes we feel like Thomas' twin as doubts bombard our faith. Another thing we don't know is where Thomas was the night of Resurrection Sunday when Jesus visited His disciples. Here's what we do know:

> **On the evening of that day, the first day of the week, the doors being locked where the disciples were for fear of the Jews, Jesus came and stood among them and said to them, "Peace be with you." When he had said this, he showed them his hands and his side. Then the disciples were glad when they saw the Lord. Jesus said to them again, "Peace be with you. As the Father has sent me, even so I am sending you." And when he had said this, he breathed on them and said to them, "Receive the Holy Spirit."[19]**

Thomas wasn't present for this surprise visit by Jesus. Sometimes we're really hard on Thomas when we really don't need to be. Yes, Thomas was absent. But earlier in the disciples' adventures with Jesus we find two really cool things about Thomas. I'm kind of sticking up for him here, on behalf of the doubters in our midst. Thomas was not some lame guy who was proud of his doubts.

In John 11, Jesus announced He was going to Bethany to

raise Lazarus, even though it was apparent the Jewish leadership in Jerusalem was plotting to kill Him. The disciples didn't like the idea. But Thomas spoke up. **"So Thomas, called the Twin, said to his fellow disciples, 'Let us also go, *that we may die with Him*.'"**[20] This guy was committed to the Lord, but he had doubts—and a good dose of pessimism.

Later, in John 14:1–6, we find the great passage, **"Let not your hearts be troubled. . . . I go to prepare a place for you. . . . I am the way. . . . No one comes to the Father except through me."** In verse 5, **"Thomas said to him, 'Lord, we do not know where you are going. How can we know the way?'"** He's so straight-up. I love people like this. He is saying, "Question! I don't get it!" Those kinds of questions were one reason Jesus, the Master Teacher, loved Thomas. Jesus wanted to make things clear. Thomas was honest enough to say, "I'm not tracking with You. What do You mean exactly?" So Thomas, even with his doubts, had a special role in the circle around Jesus.

When Jesus died, Thomas must have been devastated. How many times did he pace the floor between His death and a week later when proof of the resurrection was personally given to him? Consider the grief he felt and the regrets he had for abandoning Jesus in the garden. He must have doubted the future and wondered about the promises of Jesus. At that point, was Thomas a disillusioned doubter? Was he a disappointed doubter? I'm not sure exactly.

While we have Thomas and the other stunned disciples in mind, I want to point out five lessons about faith that overcomes doubt. These are located in John 20:24–28. This is the good news part of this chapter. I'm going to compare building faith to building a fire. You may be an expert with charcoal and firewood or a danger with matches, but realize there are some principles about faith that parallel fire building.

1. Faith is dead when the heart is passive.

Doubt flourishes when the heart isn't engaged. So many people have passive hearts. They're not actively seeking. Faith has to be cultivated. It doesn't just show up. Get a bunch of faithless, passive people together and all you have is a pile of firewood. It may be ready to burn, but lifeless hearts with no spark of faith won't ignite into flames.

You may think, *Oh, I wish I was one of those people who have deep faith. I'm just not one of those faith people.* Actually, you are not doing what faith people do in order to have more faith. You are just like a person who is in the middle of a room watching everything that's happening, but you're not part of it. Being a spectator of life isn't really living; watching faith in action isn't practicing faith.

A lot of people come to church as detached observers. The Word is going out. The worship is going up. Lives are being transformed. It's all happening, but they're simply doing their own thing. They wonder, "Why don't I have any faith?" Because they don't enter in—that's why. If you sit in your church and critique, analyze, and discard everything you see and hear, you're left with nothing. For whatever reason, you're working at doubt. You're not working at faith.

Thomas proves, in the end, to have sincere faith. If Thomas had been with the rest of the disciples on Resurrection Day, he would have seen Jesus. His doubts would have vanished. His faith would have soared. Where does John 20:19–23 tell us Thomas was that morning? It doesn't. We don't know. But he wasn't in the place where his faith would have flourished. What was he doing? Was he asleep? Did he stay up too late and miss church? Maybe *that's* what it was—the first day of the week. Notice, **"On the evening of that day, the first day of the week . . ."**[21] This was Sunday One.

"You missed Sunday Number One?"

"Yeah, I was playing cards with my friends. I got to bed kind of late. I—"

We don't know what Thomas would say. "I had to work." Was he golfing? Was he watching the pregame show? That's what TiVo is for. Was he making Sunday dinner? Was he working in his garden? We do know these are things that cause us to miss out on what God is doing among His people. Whatever it was, the rest of the disciples were there; Thomas wasn't.

Realize this: complaining about persistent doubts—if you are never in the place where faith is built—is like complaining about the darkness in your basement under a blanket with the lights off. If you want faith, you've got to get to the places where faith flourishes.

"Where does faith flourish?" you ask. Let me tell you where:

• *Faith flourishes in the Word of God.*

Romans 10:17 tells us, **"Faith comes by hearing . . . the word of God."**[22] People come to church with their heart down and discouraged and leave with their faith lifted by exposure to God's Word. That's why we come: to hear the Word of God. Strengthened faith is one of the by-products of Word-informed, Christ-centered worship.

• *Faith flourishes with the people of God.*

Friendship with people of faith increases our faith. If you don't have relationships with people of faith, you are undermining your own faith. As we showed in the last chapter with Peter's life, when surrounded by doubters, doubting comes easily. So many people live among doubters.

"I can't get away from it at work."

But are you in a small group? Are you intentionally connected with other people of faith? Are you fellowshiping with Christians? When you have an evening to spare, who do you get with? What do you talk about?

Hebrews 10:24 says, **"Let us consider how to stir up one another to love and good works."** I hope the result of every page you read here is a stirring inside; a churning and burning of faith within you. That's what I'm going for in this book.

• *Faith flourishes in the household of God.*

Going to church is a continual exercise in faith strengthening. On special weekends at Harvest, like Easter, attendance swells in our campuses to almost twenty thousand. But it almost invariably drops significantly the following week. Why?

Because at least several thousand people will think, "I was just there last week!" They are missing an important weekly dose of faith.

Jesus said, **"According to your faith be it done to you."**[23] Why does your faith struggle so much? I'm trying to tell you why.

Faith flourishes in a Book, with a group of people, at a place. Go to church. Go every week. Don't just make it a habit; make it your lifestyle. Some people object, "But my church is so stale!" Well, make sure the problem isn't with your attitude. Then, if God isn't attending your church, find one where He does show up! God is rocking the house every week somewhere near you. Go meet Him and have your faith charged up!

Hebrews 10:25 says, **"Not neglecting to meet together, as is the habit of some, but encouraging one another."** Don't forsake or neglect gathering with other believers. Thomas—he just skipped church. Whatever his reasons, it was not his best decision.

But watch Thomas' faith begin to grow in John 20:24–25, **"Now Thomas, one of the Twelve . . . was not with them when Jesus came. So the other disciples told him, 'We have seen the Lord.'"** Actually the Greek verb tense means, "they kept on saying: 'We've seen the Lord.'" It's kind of hard to be a Thomas. You know what it's like when you've missed the memo. The other disciples kept saying, "We saw the Lord. We saw the Lord!" They were egging him on a little: "How could you have missed it, Thomas? Here's your problem—we were there; you weren't!"

Thomas' answer may strike us as odd, but we will find out it wasn't prideful. **"But he said to them, 'Unless I see in his hands the mark of the nails, and place my finger into the mark of the nails, and place my hand into his side, I will never believe.'"**[24] Some people have been very harsh about Thomas' words. "Well, he seems kind of demanding and disrespectful," and "Who does he think he is?" But if we look at John 20:20, we discover an important detail in Jesus' original appearance: **"When he had said this, he showed them his hands and his side."** Thomas was only asking for what he had missed. He was expressing a willingness to believe based upon the same evidence given to the people around him. His request was not unreasonable! He didn't *want* to doubt; he wanted to believe! Thomas just longed what other people had experienced. Now that is fantastic. He was on his way to faith.

2. Faith is kindled when the heart identifies the obstacle.

Thomas is sincere. He wants to believe. He's gathering the wood. He's getting a match. He wants a faith on fire. Now he has named the obstacle. This is the most important part of this lesson. Faith is kindled when you name the obstacle.

Say what that obstacle to faith is in your life. "I got hurt. I have a question I don't have an answer for. I'm discouraged. I don't honestly understand how Christianity can be true." Name the obstacle: "Lord, *this* is the barrier between You and me." But you have to be sincere. You must really want to know. And, trust me on this one, there *is* an answer. God will go a long way in revealing Himself to a person who really wants to know.

The moment you name the obstacle, faith is going to start growing in you. It's counterintuitive but true. If you're a doubter—I challenge you to name the obstacle. What is it exactly? Produce your strong reasons and give God an opportunity to put faith where there's doubt.

I have often heard people say, "I finally became open to faith when I admitted my life was empty and out of control." Here's a great prayer to pray: "God, if You're real, prove Yourself real to me." I don't mean throw it over your shoulder as a casual challenge. I mean get on your knees every night before you go to bed—if you're a doubter—and pray this prayer from your heart: "I don't know if You're listening, but if You're real, prove Yourself real to me. I want to know. I want to see You work." God will *not* disappoint that approach. You pray that every day for thirty days. He will *meet* you at that place. I challenge you to do it sincerely. He will not let you down.

Here's the next step.

3. Faith is sparked when the Lord reveals Himself at our point of need.

Faith is sparked; ignited! Once you name the obstacle, the Lord will begin to reveal Himself to you. Jesus did not have to be told what Thomas had said. He knew. Isn't it interesting? We see no record here of other disciples reporting Thomas' refusal to believe their experience with Jesus, "Lord, here's what he said. He said that unless . . ." No. Jesus knew what he said.

As He did with Peter, Jesus answered in His timing. Thomas had to wait. **"Eight days later, his disciples were inside again, and Thomas was with them."**[25] The doubter made sure he put himself in a place of faith. "I'm going to be there. I'm going to wait for my chance."

John 20:26 goes on, **"Although the doors were locked, Jesus came and stood among them and said, 'Peace be with you.'"** Notice the precision here. Compare verses 25 and 27: **"Then he said to Thomas, 'Put your finger here, and see my hands, and put out your hand, and place it in my side.'"** Those were exactly the words Thomas used. Did Jesus understand Thomas' obstacle? He did. And He answered in a way that got things settled in Thomas' heart.

If you name the obstacle blocking faith, the Lord will meet you and reveal Himself to you at the place of your doubt. He will put faith there. But you must go *after* it. You can't have a passive, take-me-over-God, just-come-and-find-me-over-here attitude. That's not going to work. Faith is dead when the heart is passive, but it's kindled when you name the obstacle. And it is sparked when the Lord meets you and reveals Himself to you at that point in need. That tiny, hot ember of faith falls into the firewood.

4. Faith is ignited when the heart submits to the revelation.
Notice how Thomas submitted to the revelation God arranged. Jesus told him, **"Do not disbelieve, but believe"** (v. 27), implying there's a choice. **"Thomas answered him, 'My Lord and**

my God!' " (v. 28). Isn't that response awesome? One moment Thomas was thinking, "I don't get it. I don't see it." Then Jesus showed up and the doubter immediately said, "I get it. I see it! My Lord and my God!" His faith was ignited.

Notice Thomas' expression: **"my Lord."** By this phrase he meant, "My Rightful Ruler, my Master, my Sovereign, King of my life, I crown You now." He was pulling out all the stops on submission. Then he added, **"my God"**; meaning, "Beyond me, above me, uniquely different than me, and worthy of my worship and adoration." **"My Lord and my God!"** expresses beautifully Thomas' complete surrender to Christ. Now faith is on fire.

A moment like Thomas' is what it's going to take for you, doubter. You've got to submit to the revelation God brings into your life. Name the obstacle. Wait for God to make Himself known. Then respond as Thomas did to God's presence in your life.

You might think, "Well what would have happened if Jesus had shown up, scars and all, and then Thomas had answered, "Nah—I still don't believe"?

I've never seen that kind of rejection happen. God knows our hearts. If your heart does not desire faith, the Lord will not reveal Himself to you. If you pray, "Lord, show Yourself real to me," for thirty days—but in your heart you say, "It isn't going to happen. In fact, I don't even *want* Him to show up," He's not coming. But the Lord will go a long way in revealing Himself to an honest, sincere Thomas. But trust me on this one: heaven is not pacing back and forth over you or me. If you don't want to know and to believe, God's not going to show you very much. Your questions must include desire, longing, and sincerity.

Thomas had the "want to" of faith. His life reverberated with the same longing expressed by the father who said to Jesus, **"I believe; help my unbelief!"**[26] And his faith was set on fire. If you have no sincere interest, you will remain as you are.

Proverbs 29:1 says, **"He who . . . hardens his neck will suddenly be destroyed and that without remedy."** God is truly serious about our willingness to be convinced. Hebrews 11:6 assures us, **"And without faith it is impossible to please him, for whoever would draw near to God must believe that he exists and that he rewards those who seek him."**

5. Faith is ablaze when it comes before seeing.

An immature Christian can be expected to say, "Show me, Lord. I've got to see it." This is simple and helpless dependence. I believe that God, in His love and mercy, will show such young faith something. He will reveal Himself to an infant believer. You and I, however, want to get to the place where we don't have to see it to believe. We want to grow into followers of Jesus who can say, "I've seen enough. Christ is right. He's true. I trust. I don't have to keep asking God to reconfirm what He has shown me."

Practicing a mature faith is where we want to live our lives. That's what Jesus exhorted when He said in John 20:29, **"Have you believed because you have seen me? Blessed are those who have not seen and yet have believed."** Growing trust really fires

God up. He delights to hear His children say, "It's enough! I believe every word You say. I trust everything You tell me. I'm not going to put my questions ahead of obedience; I'm going to obey and let You settle any questions in Your time. You're God and I'm not—and I like it that way."

When you get to that place, the doubtful wanderer you once were will be a memory in your rearview mirror. You will be looking forward to where God is taking you, excited to be traveling under His direction, knowing all the while that you are actually home.

CHAPTER 4

SENSUAL
WANDERER
—COME HOME!

THIS CHAPTER, like the rest of the book, flows out of the need to take James 5:19 seriously if we are claiming ourselves to be followers of Jesus Christ:

> **My brothers, if anyone among you wanders from the truth and someone brings him back, let him know that whoever brings back a sinner from his wandering will save his soul from death and will cover a multitude of sins.**

If we carry out the passage above, sooner or later we will find ourselves approaching someone with the message, "Sensual wanderer—come home!" If that invitation sets off warning alarms in your mind, this is probably the chapter for you.

Let's begin with a good definition of the word *sensual* to avoid confusion. When I use the term *sensual,* it includes—

but is not limited to—sexual activity. The definition reveals a frequent misunderstanding of the word. Sensual is more than sexual. The word actually means *pertaining to, inclined to, or preoccupied with the gratification of my body*. Those are the basic boundaries of sensuality. The idea comes from a Latin word *sensualis* which means *of the senses; the pursuit of that which pleases my senses*. A sensual person, then, is one who is consumed with indulging his or her own desires. I want to be clear: sensual does mean sexual but also includes many other expressions of sensuality that lead to wandering. Here are some areas of sensual desire where people struggle not to be conquered.

• **Food.**

Let's start with one common to so many of us: food. Food stirs a desire that is not wrong in itself (hunger), but it can become wrong and unhealthy (craving for food). Current figures from the Centers for Disease Control (www.cdc.gov) indicate a third of the population fall into the obese category. In the two decades between 1990 and 2010, the rate of obesity increased significantly. There are many socioeconomic factors, but it is fair to say we are overweight due to eating habits. Even for the healthy, there is a growing fascination with what we consume, with entire television programing focused on stuff to eat. The craving for food can be a sensual problem.

• **Entertainment.**

Entertainment is a second category of sensuality. Americans spend more than 24 billion dollars on DVD rentals, not to mention skyrocketing amounts spent on Internet viewing and direct downloads like Netflix. Imagine the countless hours invested watching these presentations. And if that wasn't enough, the average person watches 142 hours of television per month. That much time comes out to almost a full-time job. One in seven people and increasing have an Internet addiction, spending thirty or more hours per week on nonessential online activities including games, shopping, gambling, and illicit sites. Neil Postman said it well: "We're amusing ourselves to death."[1]

• Legal Substances.

Legal substances make up a third category that attracts and exhausts people's senses. Let's start with something common—coffee; 400 billion cups of coffee are consumed every year, making caffeine the most commonly taken mind-altering drug on the planet. A Starbucks Grande—about 360 mg of caffeine—is enough to cause heightened stress and insomnia. You might wonder, "Do they know that they're making us addicted?"

"No, they have no idea." But think again before you accept that answer. Both producers and consumers of potentially dangerous items bear a responsibility for their participation, particularly when the dangers are public knowledge.

Now to a more serious legal substance: alcohol. Addiction to alcohol is absolutely tearing and shredding the fabric of our society. There isn't a social evil that is not significantly amplified by alcohol. Drill down on any problem you identify—from incest to spousal abuse to murder—and the common factor in many of these cases is alcohol. Here's why: Alcohol takes everything wrong in our hearts and turns the volume up on all of it, while drowning out the attempts of conscience to urge caution. Alcohol scrambles our senses. It may be a legal substance, but a person can have a consuming desire for something even when it's destroying them and those around them.

• Illegal Substances.

Statistics show that well over 20 million people in the United States used illegal drugs in a recent year. But those are only the ones that got caught. Marijuana was the most common forbidden drug; painkillers were second; cocaine was third. There's a lot of talk these days about how drug use among high school students is going down slightly; but interestingly, it increased by 50 percent among people over fifty years of age during the last few years. Ironically, people desire illegal drugs not to pursue heightened senses but to numb the pain of life. Young people can still be deluded into thinking an altered mental state is better; older people are disillusioned and settle for thinking that an altered mental state simply avoids worse feelings and thoughts. God doesn't want you to numb life for any reason. He wants you to deal with it with His help and power.

• Immorality: Sexual Sin.

We finally come, of course, to what we often equate with sensuality—immorality. Christianity teaches that sex is a good gift created by God and intended for pleasure and procreation within marriage. But outside the lines that God has prescribed, sex can become something wonderful used wrongly for evil. As such, it can produce very destructive results. According to the Guttmacher Institute, by the age of nineteen, three-quarters of men and women have had intercourse and more than two-thirds have had two or more sexual partners. Deviance is being defined down in our society so that less and less people consider any behavior sexually abnormal or perverse. An increasing percentage of Americans believe that cohabitation, adultery, homosexuality, and pornography are morally acceptable behaviors. Sensuality, in our culture, is out of control. What was hidden and shameful has become promoted and in some cases protected by the weight of law. What the Bible calls sin is today being hailed as wonderful personal rights not to be infringed on or even questioned by anyone.

Obviously some of the categories I've just mentioned are more serious than others. I'm not suggesting that Starbucks and sodomy are on the same plane. I *am* saying you can't sit there all smug and self-satisfied because you don't have certain sensual problems. The Scriptures say, **"I will not be brought under the power of any."**[2] I want God to be the *only* influence that reigns supreme in my life. As long as any desire for anything or anyone else is reigning in my life or yours, we are not controlled by God and we are behaving as sensually minded people.

I got a letter from a lady in our church this week—very heartfelt, precious, and tender. "Please Pastor James, don't speak about sexual sin and give the impression that men struggle with this but women do not." She included some statistics how Internet pornography usage among women is escalating almost as fast as it is among men and how this is not a male-only problem. That was a helpful word for me. In all matters of sensuality, this chapter is for every humble heart ready to listen and wanting more of the good things that God offers and less of the sinful things that consume us but never really deliver what they promise.

SAMSON, THE SENSUAL

People often know fragments about the Old Testament figure named Samson: long hair, great strength, Delilah. Samson was a sensual person. Judges 13 introduces Samson through his parents, who were barren, but were given a miracle child. An angel suddenly appeared and announced to Samson's parents, "You're going to have a boy, and he's going to be special. He's going to belong to Me from the day that he is born." So, after years of infertility, Samson's parents were fired up to worship God and do what He commanded.

Samson was raised as a Nazirite. In the Old Testament, a Nazirite was a person who took a vow to belong totally to God. Today, Christians would say we're all supposed to have taken that vow! Belonging totally to God is what the lordship of Jesus Christ is all about.

But in Old Testament days, the culture specified certain behavior to indicate God's ownership. A Nazirite vow meant that a person, first, would abstain from all wine and strong drink. It is always interesting to me how often the Bible reports that people who belong totally to God, whether it was a priest or a Nazirite, stayed away from alcohol.

Second, Nazirites were forbidden to touch a corpse—not a person, not an animal—nothing dead.

And third, they were not allowed to cut their hair for the duration of the vow, which in Samson's case was for a lifetime. These were signs to remind him of God's ownership. When he walked by a barbershop, he thought, "Nah, I belong to God." When someone would offer him a drink, he said, "No thanks, I belong to God." He was to be prompted by these little practical choices to remember, "My life belongs totally to God."

Sadly—pathetically—Samson's life did *not* belong to God; it belonged to Samson. He was a sensual person. Though he grew up under God's blessing,[3] his attention was drawn to pleasure like a moth to a sizzling bulb. It was only a matter of time before he wandered. **"Samson went down to Timnah, and at Timnah he saw one of the daughters of the Philistines."**[4] He was in the wrong place to scout for a wife. The Philistines were the archenemies of the nation of Israel. The angel who announced Samson's birth had indicated in Judges 13:5, **"he shall begin to save Israel from the hand of the Philistines."** Yet in his interaction with them, Samson's life provides a case study of the tragedy of sensual wandering.

INCOMPLETE OBEDIENCE EQUALS ONGOING PROBLEMS

Here's a further background note to Samson's story. The Philistines were among the people God instructed Joshua and Israel to remove from the Promised Land. They weren't supposed to be around. God gave Joshua all the authority and the armies to expel them. But the Israelites thought, "Why clear the land? We've got our space here. Everything's good. Let's all coexist and have a party!" Because they didn't finish the job God had given them (incomplete obedience), they lived with ongoing problems with the Philistines for generations.

The Philistines were an enemy—a deadly nuisance in the neighborhood. Samson was raised up by God and given special strengths to drive the Philistines out. But instead of using his abilities to do the job God assigned him, he used his unusual capacity to satisfy his sensual self. His failure set the stage for later disasters like the ark of the covenant being captured and the contest between David and Goliath. Those confrontations all involved the Philistines. We can see the pattern today! Incomplete obedience invites ongoing problems.

BACK TO SAMSON

So Samson—sensual guy—came back from Timnah with a Philistine girl on his mind. Judges 14:2 goes on, **"Then he came up and told his father and mother, 'I saw one of the daughters of the Philistines at Timnah.'"** Now "saw" here doesn't mean he "observed." Samson wasn't saying, "Oh, I noticed this girl." He *saw* her. His senses redlined. He was smitten.

Popular today is the notion that a preacher—in order to communicate clearly—needs to use graphic and erotic speech to come across as cool and culturally relevant. Incorrect! The

Bible, and this passage is a good example, purposely veils things so that we all get the situation without having to wallow in it. We don't need to arouse anyone in order to talk about Samson's sensual wandering. As we have already said, sex within God's boundaries is honorable. He protects it! Hebrews 13:4 says, **"Let marriage be held in honor among all, and let the marriage bed be undefiled, for God will judge the sexually immoral and adulterous."** Undefiled! But it is *private,* and not for casual or even flippant conversation. The consequences of ignoring God's protections are painful.

Even after Samson saw the Philistine girl, he could have walked away. Instead he plunged into wandering when he told his parents in Judges 14:2, **"Now get her for me as my wife."** Here we can begin to see in Samson the profile of a sensual wanderer.

Sensual wanderers have no respect. Judges 14:1–7

Despite his remarkable upbringing, Samson displayed a stunning lack of respect. The word *respect* means *to esteem; to show deference to a person of value who is worthy of honor.* Samson developed no proper respect. It's not hard to imagine how a previously barren couple who had been blessed by God began to enable their only son's self-indulgence. It was difficult for them to say *no* to their special child, but that was their job. I'm sure the first time Samson pulled a trick like this they were torn and tearful. But somehow they learned to make peace by giving Samson just what he wanted. They were enabling his sensual self-destruction. And we see the tragic results:

- Samson had no respect for God, so God used his sensual wandering to accomplish His purposes. Judges 14:4 describes God's work behind the scenes. **"His father and mother did not know that it was from the LORD, for he was seeking an opportunity against the Philistines. At that time the Philistines ruled over Israel."** Now, isn't that amazing? Even though Samson was so sensual and evil, God used his wickedness to advance His own purposes. Isn't that the way it is, though? If I do right, God uses me. If I do wrong, God uses me. God is going to always make sure that what God wants to have happen, happens.

- Samson had no respect for God's law. He was about to seek a wife outside Israel.

- Samson had no respect for the calling that God had placed on his life. Even the strength he used to kill a lion (vv. 5–6) didn't cause him to stop and think. He knew what was forbidden, but he *wanted* what was forbidden. And nothing was going to stop him. He was a sensual person.

- Samson had no respect for his parents, for their feelings, for their objections. "They're in the way!" He callously cast them aside to please himself.

- Samson had no genuine respect for himself. He was a man called and gifted by God. He had an incredible opportunity to bless others. Instead, his goal became to satisfy his sensual self. Nothing was going to get in the way.

Samson had no respect. Or to be technically correct, he had a sensually distorted respect. He *did* show deference to his own desires. He exercised esteem and gave honor to his sensual self at the expense of his true self. Sensual wanderers exhibit a lack of respect.

Sensual wanderers are controlled by their appetite. Judges 14:8–9

Although Samson had remarkable capabilities, he allowed himself to be controlled by his appetites. Like all sensual wanderers, Samson's life was out of control. Judges 14:8 reports, **"After some days he returned to take her."** Notice, Samson didn't return to woo her or to win her affections; he didn't ask or invite. For the sensual wanderer, people are always things to be used. "People are props in my personal drama. They're options on my car as I race down the carefree highway," says the sensual wanderer.

You may not realize how often, and in what different forms, self-centeredness shows up in our lives. Did it ever occur to you that your obesity is injuring your spouse's capacity to be attracted to you? Did you ever think that your addiction to mood-altering substances is dulling the pain of things your loved ones long for you to deal with? Do you realize that your family knows more about your Internet addiction than you might imagine? More than they have the courage to talk to you about, for fear that you'll go over the edge if they try to help you change? For the sensual wanderer, the answer to these questions is *no*. The sensual wanderer hears only one voice—appetite: "What I want. What I need to feed my sensual self."

Judges 14:8 continues, **"And he turned aside to see the carcass of the lion, and behold, there was a swarm of bees in the body of the lion, and honey,"** to which Samson should have responded, "Ugh!" because as a Nazirite he knew he was not allowed to touch dead things. But that didn't matter to him. He had a hunger! He needed a sugar fix! So, **"He scraped it out into his hands and went on, eating as he went. And he came to his father and mother and gave some to them, and they ate. But he did not tell them that he had scraped the honey from the carcass of the lion"** (v. 9). So not only did he sin himself, he also ceremonially defiled his parents. Why did God's law not stop Samson? Why did he not say to himself, "Oh! That's wrong! I can't do that"? Because he was a sensual person who had only learned to feed his appetite—never to deny it.

Not long ago I was talking with one of my best friends in ministry Jack Graham, who pastors Prestonwood Baptist Church in Dallas. Since we are both grandfathers, it's fun to share stories about our grandchildren. Jack told me about taking his little grandson, Ian, then about four years old, to a baseball game. One of the Texas Rangers is Ian's absolute favorite player. When the player came up to the plate, this little boy yelled out as loud as he could from the stands, "Do what ya want! Do what ya want out there!" It was so funny, imagining this kid coaching a professional athlete, "You do whatever ya want out there!" I laughed so hard when I heard that story . . . and then I thought again. That expression captures what the sensual wanderer says when a situation reminds him of God's instruction—"Samson! God's law!"

He responds, "I do what *I* want out there. Should I eat this cake? Should I drink this six-pack? Should I watch this video? I do what *I* want. Why should today be any different?" Sensual wanderers are controlled by appetite.

Sensual wanderers are oblivious to the carnage. Judges 14:10–15:20

Sensual wanderers are just flat-out blind to the impact their choices are making on others. If you have felt the pain of loving a sensual wanderer, you've probably asked yourself, "Don't they see the damage they're doing?" The answer is no. Others are a channel the sensual wanderer never tunes in to. They can't hear, see, or feel beyond their own desires.

The rest of Judges 14 describes Samson's wedding to this woman. In those times they had a seven-day wedding feast. We can hardly imagine a weeklong wedding reception. They would go day after day, partying. At the end of the seventh day, the couple would consummate the marriage, and then the two were considered married. He would have called her his wife, but they had not come together until the end of the seventh day. That will help you understand the passage.

Samson gave them a riddle as part of the feast:

"Out of the eater came something to eat.

Out of the strong came something sweet."[5]

Then he said, "I'll make you a bet. If you can tell me the answer to that riddle—what am I talking about—by the last day of the feast, then I'll get you thirty pieces of linen and thirty changes of clothing. If you can't tell me, then you've got to get those items for me."

They took the bet, but they had a plan. **"On the fourth day** (of the seven) **they said to Samson's wife, 'Entice your husband to tell us what the riddle is, lest we burn you and your father's house with fire' "** (v. 15). Faced with such a threat, the bride thought, "I'm going to try enticing my husband. That would be a lot better than our houses going up in flames."

So she worked Samson over with weeping, sighing, and comments like, "You hate me. You don't love me. Tell me the riddle." For a while, Samson held his ground. But she persisted. **"And on the seventh day he told her, because she pressed him hard"** (v. 17). Even in this situation, given a choice between integrity under pressure or satisfaction, Samson made the sensual choice. Anyone who understood the chink in his armor could control him.

No sooner had Samson confided in his bride than she passed on the answer: **"Then she told the riddle to her people. And the men of the city said to him on the seventh day before the sun went down,**

'What is sweeter than honey?

What is stronger than a lion?'

And he said to them, 'If you had not plowed with my

heifer, you would not have found out my riddle'" (v. 18). What a statement! Now he should have said to himself, "Yeah, this pagan lady is probably never going to be on my team. It's fairly obvious that she's going to be here for her family and not for me. I should have figured out what was going on behind her demands." But that's not what he did. Instead he got furiously angry. He went out and killed thirty men, stripped off their clothes, and delivered them to those who had solved the riddle. Samson took no lessons away from that disaster. The sensual person is one of the hardest people to teach because the lessons are quickly forgotten when desire comes knocking. They get stunningly forgetful. They are oblivious to the carnage they are causing even in their own lives.

Judges 15 continues the story some time later. **"After some days, at the time of wheat harvest, Samson went to visit his wife with a young goat"** (v. 1). It's hard to imagine showing up on Valentine's Day and saying to our wives, "Honey, I love you, so I got you this goat." But we have to remember that one culture's dozen roses and a box of chocolates is another culture's goat. This was romance Philistine style.

Notice the verse indicates a few days had passed. The sensual wanderer always comes out of the stupor eventually and awakes to the mess he has made. He may even regret what the pleasure cost. By going back to this woman, Samson was really saying, "I want my sin and I want my way." Sensual wanderers always claim rights and expect no consequences. They make statements like, "I want my sin *and* my health"; "I want my sin *and* my family"; "I want my sin *and* my ministry." The bottom line for the sensual wanderer doesn't include turning away from sin; it always retains the sin and wants more. He admits, "When push comes to shove between pleasure and good, I'm going to take what satisfies me. But, I'm really trying to have *both*." They can't see they are destroying the one to get the other—either way.

Even when trying to make a correction, Samson quickly reverted to his demanding self. He did show up with a goat to make peace and resume a relationship, but he said, **" 'I will go in to my wife in the chamber.' But her father would not allow him to go in"** (v. 1). Here's the problem. At the end of the betrothal—when they were supposed to consummate the marriage—Samson was away killing thirty people to meet his clothing obligation, so the family would have been shamed by the groom's absence. So the father gave his daughter to the best man. And when the strongest guy in the universe showed up again, he didn't like the bad news. Sensual wanderers do not like bad news, especially you-can't-have-what-you-want news.

Judges 15:**2** describes the father's hasty explanation. **"And her father said, 'I really thought that you utterly hated her, so I gave her to your companion. Is not her younger sister more beautiful than she? Please take her instead.' "** We can read between the lines, "Don't hurt me, please!" The father knew Samson had killed thirty people to get some clothes, so he feared for his life.

"And Samson said to them, 'This time I shall be inno-

cent in regard to the Philistines' " (v. 3). He went off crazy again! And he blamed everyone else beforehand for what he was about to do.

"Why so angry when the pretty sister was offered?" Because he wasn't rational—he was sensual. His was not a thoughtful or logical response; it was a loins and sensual thing. It was a feeling reaction: "I want what I want. Get out of my way!" This is the life of the sensual wanderer. "What I desire is my idol. It's in my heart and I *have* to have it." That kind of thinking shatters sincerity. It ruins reason. And the worst part of it was his blindness to his destructive, wandering pattern.

In a rage, Samson went on a rampage using foxes dragging torches as weapons of mass destruction. This caused the death of his wife and in-laws. Then he killed a thousand Philistines, which brought him to a point of physical exhaustion. Completely spent, he finally turned to God, only to demand, "You gave me this victory. Now I'm thirsty. God, get me some water!" God graciously opened a rock, and water flowed to meet his need. But it didn't curb his sensual pursuit. He couldn't see the carnage he was leaving in his wake.

Sensual wanderers are getting worse and growing weaker. Judges 16:1–19

The story of a sensual wanderer does not plateau or retrace its steps back home. If you are wandering from God into some form of sensuality, it's worse now than it was two months ago. It's feeding on itself. You may think, "I'm managing my sin."

No; it's managing you. And it's getting worse.

We rejoin Samson at Judges 16:1: **"Samson went to Gaza, and there he saw a prostitute, and he went in to her."** The writer of Scripture is not surprised. Samson saw a prostitute and decided on the spot to have her. Two chapters ago he got his parents and his wife's parents involved; not now. Not to the increasingly sensual wanderer. Again he "saw" her. He went. He wanted. He took. He felt. He got. It's his new normal. Samson went into the prostitute's house.

We don't know what he might have said if someone had confronted him. "Samson! You're God's man. You're God's *man*. What are you doing?" But his actions indicate what he might have said: "Hey, I thought I was going to be married. I have needs! Leave me alone. End of discussion." People were watching Samson, however, and they thought his decision to visit the prostitute presented an opportunity to destroy him. Judges 16:2–3 continues the story:

> **The Gazites were told, "Samson has come here." And they surrounded the place and set an ambush for him all night at the gate of the city. They kept quiet all night, saying, "Let us wait till the light of the morning; then we will kill him." But Samson lay till midnight, and at midnight he arose and took hold of the doors of the gate of the city and the two posts, and pulled them up, bar and all, and put them on his shoulders and carried them to the top of the hill that is in front of Hebron.**

I remember hearing this story when I was a kid and thinking, "That's dumb. Samson, what are you doing?"

"Well I saw these gates. And I thought I could probably lift 'em! Nobody *else* can pick them up, but I can. I'm the strongest man. So I carried 'em up the hill and left them there!" `

Even as a youngster, I thought, "You're a silly clown, Samson. Your gifts and abilities are for God. You're supposed to be using your strength to drive out the Philistines and you're using it to entertain them. All you ever think about is what pleases you."

In Judges 16:4 the plot in Samson's life thickens significantly. **"After this he loved a woman in the Valley of Sorek."** She may have been an Israelite; this was a border region that changed hands almost yearly between the Philistines and Israel. Her name was Delilah.

"And the lords of the Philistines came up to her and said to her, 'Seduce him, and see where his great strength lies, and by what means we may overpower him, that we may bind him to humble him. And we will each give you 1,100 pieces of silver' " (v. 5). It would appear she was an Israelite, because if she was a Philistine, they wouldn't have had to pay her. They would have told her this was a case of national security.

"So Delilah said to Samson, 'Please tell me where your great strength lies, and how you might be bound, that one could subdue you' " (v. 6). What follows between Samson, Delilah, and the Philistines is a deadly cat-and-mouse game. Let me say this: men who use their strength to intimidate and manipulate women are wicked! You are practicing wickedness if the abilities God intended you to use to cover and protect your family are used instead to get your sensual way. This is also true: women who use sex to control and convince men are also wicked. It is also wickedness if rather than using the gift that God gave you to embrace the man to whom you are married, you use it to deceive or manipulate.

Judges 16:5–22 records three rounds of the dangerous game: "I'll give you what you want if you give me what I want." It's all implied in the text. You don't have to be brilliant to see it. It turns into a wicked contest between sensual people. For all his physical strength, Samson was a moral and sensual weakling.

Women who catch their man through sexual ensnarement end up married to a sensual person! The strategy may work, but the results are often tragic. Women who use their sexuality to trap a man end up married to a self-centered person may wonder, "How did my life become this?"

Samson participated in his own destruction. At first he played along with Delilah. He wanted what she had, so he told her, "The kryptonite for me is fresh bowstrings. Tie me up with those, " **'then I shall become weak'"** (v. 7). Actually Samson, you're already weak. You don't even know it. So she bound him with bowstrings. Judges 16:9 describes the results: **"Now she had men lying in ambush in an inner chamber. And she said to him, 'The Philistines are upon you, Samson!' But he snapped the bowstrings, as a thread of flax snaps when it touches the fire."** Though temporarily deterred, Delilah redoubled her efforts. She chided Samson for lying to her. " **'Please** tell me how you might be bound.' And he said to her, 'If they bind me with new ropes that have not been used . . .' So Delilah took new ropes and bound him with them and said to him, 'The Philistines are upon you, Samson!' " (vv. 10–11). But Samson escaped again.

In the next round, Samson revealed his strength had something to do with his hair. His uncut locks were part of his Nazirite vow. This partial revelation indicated he was weakening. When Delilah followed the instructions he had given her, braiding his hair in a loom and anchoring it to the pin, the results were the same as the first two times.

I haven't had a ton of experience with hair lately, but how does a person sleep through having their hair braided in such a painful way? He was playing along or simply was at that sensual place where he was no longer in his right mind. Such a person has reached an advanced self-destruct mode. At this point, the sensual person does not need assistance from alcohol or anything else; he is already a train wreck.

Having failed three times, Delilah was determined. She turned up the manipulation dial all the way. She replayed her three disappointments and insisted she wouldn't be satisfied until she knew his secret. What was wrong with Samson? Are we to believe he didn't realize he was being played? She had all these Philistines hiding down behind the couch ready to pounce when they found out he wasn't strong enough—at least that's the way I always pictured it when I was a kid.

As we read the final round of the game, we want to shout

a warning to Samson: "Don't tell her!" But she closes in and he folds. **"'You have mocked me these three times, and you have not told me where your great strength lies.' And when she pressed him hard with her words day after day, and urged him** (some translations say *pestered* or *nagging*)**, his soul was vexed . . ."** (vv. 15–16). *Vexed* means *bothered* or *annoyed.* It means literally *it was cut short*. He just didn't have the strength to keep the game going.

"**And he told her all his heart, and said to her, 'A razor has never come upon my head, for I have been a Nazirite to God from my mother's womb' "** (v. 17). Now he totally opens the war chest and gives her everything *she* wants so he can get everything *he* wants. She realized immediately she had broken through his last defenses. She summoned his enemies and prepared him for betrayal.

Judges 16:19 describes the process, **"She made him sleep on her knees."** Delilah was ready when Samson took his afterpleasure nap. "Okay, you've told me what I want. Now you can have what you want. Now go to sleep." **"And she called a man and had him shave off the seven locks of his head."** When the barber was done, **"She began to torment him."** Delilah wasn't confused or ambivalent about this situation. She *enjoyed* winning this deadly game. Her own sensual lusts needed to be satisfied, and defeating Samson must have been thrilling for her.

She wasn't standing when the Philistines rushed in and gouged his eyes out, crying, "Oh! I love him! Don't hurt him!" She had been tormenting him to wake him up—it means to profane him. She was mocking him, "In your face now, strong boy!" She was hateful toward him. And he was so naïve, so blinded by his sensual focus, that he never saw the betrayal until his eyes were being destroyed. Now he was a pathetic shell of a man.

Notice how the progression unfolds here. Living for pleasure pulls you in as it is increasingly dissatisfying. It takes more calories to get a sugar high. More alcohol must be consumed to get in a stupor. Greater exposure to pornography or something more perverse is required to get a sexual high.

Sensual wanderers get worse and grow weaker. Is that you? The sensual wanderer thinks, "I'll get close to the edge of the cliff and then I'll stop. I won't go over." After thirty years of pastoral ministry, I can tell you what happens when they get close to the edge. They hit the gas pedal—that's what they do. They give up all pretense of desire for right and good. "Oh well, I can't live this in-between thing anymore." Far from stopping, they accelerate toward their own destruction. I wish I could tell you that's not what happens. But if you still care, stop the vehicle that is your life while you can, because I don't enjoy telling you this last phase of a wanderer's journey.

Sensual wanderers will be abandoned by God Himself. Judges 16:20–22

Just as the father had to let the prodigal go—not because he wanted to, but because he had to,[6] God has certain responses to our deliberate wandering. Some people insist on eating pig food to find out how bad it tastes. So God the Father sometimes lets us go to learn the futility of life without Him.

Having mentioned God's abandonment, let me point out that the pursuit of pleasure is not the core sin. God does not want us to live a cheerless, pleasureless existence. He has a full life in mind for us!

One of the greatest books written in our lifetime is the slim volume by John Piper called *Desiring God*. If you are a sensual wanderer, you absolutely must read this book. It makes the point that we were made to desire pleasure. The unexpected twist in our design is that genuine, lasting pleasure can only be found in God. Pleasure seeking is the way He made us. It's not the desire that's wrong; the wrong comes when sin causes us to desire wrongly. Wanting to be pleased, wanting to be satisfied, wanting to experience joy is not sin. It's the substitutes to God as the true source of pleasure that are the sin.

Piper subtitled his book *Confessions of a Christian Hedonist*. Hedonism is the pursuit of pleasure. He explains we were made to find our greatest soul happiness and delight in God. The shocking solution for the sensual wanderer is not "Stop it!" That's not it. Here's what it is: finding the joy that your heart is longing for in the One who made you for Himself— the Savior who died and rose again to give you a life you can never find on your own. God doesn't want to take pleasure from you. He wants to give it to you. Every time God says, "Don't," He's really saying, "Don't hurt yourself. I love you. Chasing your own pleasures is not going to do it for you. You need Me." Find your pleasure in God alone.

How sad that Samson, who was raised to live a life in God and for God, lived so far apart and yet so precariously close to the one thing that he truly needed. Eventually God would say, "Do you think your way is better than Me? You've got to have that? Then go have it."

Judges 16:**20** begins the stunning final chapter in Samson's life. **"And she said, 'The Philistines are upon you, Samson!' And he awoke from his sleep and said, 'I will go out as at other times and shake myself free.' "** He didn't see the boulder about to land on his head. When you're falling into sensual pleasure, you think, "I can shake myself free at any point. I'm not going to get caught in this sin." And for a time it appears you can succeed. Eventually, however, the sensual quest takes control and you can't get away. Sin desires to have you. Sin desires to rule over you. For a time, Samson could shake himself free and do something for God. But eventually he came to the place where God gave him over to his pursuit. Suddenly God's grace was no longer stirring in his heart. And he couldn't shake himself free.

One of the saddest phrases in the Old Testament is the end of Judges 16:20, **"But he did not know that the LORD had left him."** He didn't realize it. He didn't feel the vacuum. He didn't know the Lord had removed His power.

You might say, "Are you trying to scare me, James?"

Yes, I am. If there is still time for you to be scared, I want you to be terrified. If you don't make a decision about this before you close this book, I want you to have a sleepless night. I want you to toss and turn until you take that computer and throw it in the dumpster. You can't tiptoe out of a sensual life; it takes the radical turnaround the Bible calls *repentance*. Jesus said in Matthew 5:29–30, **"If your right eye causes you to sin, tear it out and throw it away. For it is better that you lose one of your members than that your whole body be thrown into hell. And if your right hand causes you to sin, cut it off and throw it away. For it is better that you lose one of your members than that your whole body go into hell."** Getting right with God takes serious hand-eye coordination, including tears and letting go of stuff we want to keep seeing and holding.

The sensual wanderer will eventually be abandoned by God Himself. If you ask, "Is there still time for me?" I can say, based on the grace of Christ, "Yes, if you care, there is." But repentance will cut you all the way to the bone. You will have to let go of everything that isn't of God from your old life.

Has the boulder of reality fallen on you? Is that why you're wondering if there's a chance? Samson lost everything before he realized he could have the one thing that really mattered. Judges 16:21 says, **"And the Philistines seized him and gouged out his eyes and brought him down to Gaza and bound him with bronze shackles. And he ground at the mill in the prison."** Is it over for him? It looked like it. It may seem that way in your life right now. But if you are still reading this, there's hope. It wasn't too late for Samson and it isn't too late for you. When Samson's life had been reduced to a grind in the dark, things may have seemed hopeless for a while, **"But the hair of his head began to grow again"** (v. 22). The symbol of his heart toward God began to return.

It's not too late for sensual wanderers to come home. Judges 16:23–31

The clock might be winding down, but it's not too late. With all your sin, all your shame, all your defeat, and all your addictions—it's not too late.

You know, not being able to see may have been the greatest mercy to Samson as a sensual wanderer. He couldn't see stuff anymore as he trudged in that mill grinding 'round and 'round. Maybe being in that prison was the best thing that happened to him because his feet couldn't wander after sensuality. God in His mercy put Samson on lockdown! He had a lot of time to think about who he was and what he had become.

Given their shared history, the Philistines hated Samson. His story ends when he was brought to a big party so the Philistines could mock him and make sport of him. This may have been weeks or months or years later, but it wasn't a couple of days. His hair had grown back, but he couldn't see. They led him up where they could ridicule him in some way. As the Philistines jeered, he said to the servant leading him, "Let me feel the pillars" (v. 26). There were three thousand people up on the roof. Samson prayed, **"'O Lord God, please remember me and please strengthen me only this once, O God, that I may be avenged on the Philistines for my two eyes'"** (v. 28). His final request strikes us as sad. How about avenged for disgracing God? Or avenged for destroying your life? How about avenged for denying your mission? But for his eyes? Yet God in grace answered him.

Question: Was Samson repentant? I don't know if he was. I don't think we're allowed to make a judgment. There's not enough evidence. Better we answer for *our* lives than his.

But here's a note that blows me away: Hebrews 11:32 lists Samson as a man of faith. It's not too late for the sensual wanderer. You don't have to say, "Well, this is the way I am. I'm never going to be different." You *can* be different—not by your own power, but by God's power released in you by the Holy Spirit if you will surrender to Him.

I don't want to end this chapter by letting you off the hook if you are considering your current condition as a wanderer. Please read these closing thoughts prayerfully. Revelation 3:20 begins, **"Behold, I stand at the door and knock."** The older I get, the more I realize there just aren't a ton of opportunities like this moment. If you have been a sensual person for weeks, months, or years in one of these ways we have been examining, you know there haven't been many chances to turn, to really see where you're at and the gap between where you are and where you want to be. You don't know if this might be your last.

In just a moment I want you to close this book and sit quietly before God. He knows everything about you—more than you know about yourself. I know there's a lot of shame involved with sensual sin. We don't want to add *shame* for you. God *loves* you. We want you to get free. When you close the book, think about the Lord's patient and loving pursuit, standing and knocking, inviting you to open the door. If you can't see it immediately, ask Him to show you. Make a big change. God may be using this chapter as a wake-up boulder in your life, but I suspect if this is your moment, something larger is looming or has crushed you. This is the crisis that can be your turning point. Ask God to take it all, all the dark and dirt and shame that His Son already died for in your life, and to forgive you and set you free. Come home, wanderer, come home.

Either before or after you spend time before God, read the prayer below because it may help you frame your conversation with Him:

God, thank You that in Your mercies and by Your Spirit You see every person reading this right now. You know us intimately. We have wandered into a far country for too long. We have spent far too much on that which does not satisfy. And we long to be changed.

I pray, God, beyond the crisis of this decision, to be different, that there wouldn't be a momentary strengthening and then a lapsing further into sensuality. I pray instead there would be strong moves; steps to put different kinds of content into my mind; moves to put different kinds of supportive relationships into my life; moves to actually cut off any opportunity that there might be to pursue old patterns of sensuality. Your Word says, "Make no provision for the flesh."[6] And God, You know the places where we fail; the places we go; the things we see; the access we have to that which neither pleases You nor satisfies us. Forgive us, Lord.

So we pray by Your Spirit, God, that You would give us courage to make big decisions. Life is short and eternity is long. Give us courage, strength, and purity—not legalism—but purity. Not just doing right things, but desiring right things; finding in Jesus Christ all that our hearts are longing for. Never have we followed You and regretted that decision. Often we have wandered and felt the pain of living apart from You. Welcome us home.

So I pray in the strong name of Jesus that You would set this reader free today, God; that You would take the scales off of his or her eyes; that You would release his or her spirit from the bondage that has brought such misery and shame; and that You would wash over him or her in this moment with grace and mercy and forgiveness. How great is Your love toward us!

In Jesus' name, Amen.

CHAPTER 5

WILLFUL
WANDERER
—COME HOME!

THIS IS THE FINAL CHAPTER on wanderers. We've talked about Doubtful Wanderers, Fearful Wanderers, and Sensual Wanderers. This next character is the hardest wanderer to deal with. As with each of the wanderers we've met, this one is also someone we should be going to get in response to James 5:19–20. I call this person the Willful Wanderer. Biblically, we would call him or her a prodigal.

When we think of a prodigal, we often picture a young person. But sometimes prodigals turn out to be in their thirties, forties, or fifties, and it's not their parents they are leaving, it's their marriage or their extended family. Willful wanderers know what they are doing, but they are determined to do it no matter what good reasons they are given to stay where they are.

There are many kinds of prodigals. But I believe there are not many things that touch families as deeply and painfully as prodigals do. There is probably not a family in our church that doesn't have a prodigal somewhere in their extended relationships. These wanderers are all around us, and it breaks our hearts.

Even though this chapter is focused on calling prodigals home, I find it hard as a pastor not to think about how these words will be read and felt by those whose hearts are heavy for prodigals. I was sitting at the piano yesterday thinking about how helpless we often feel when we're waiting for wanderers to come home. I started playing a song I haven't played for a long time. It's called "In His Time." It talks about how we can commit the burdens on our heart to God and that God's going to work it out in His time—not our time. But in His time. The song is easy to find on YouTube and probably familiar to you. The words speak into everything that lies between you and God right now—people, situations, needs that are waiting on His timing. Will you let God pour trust into your life as you wait on Him?

Luke 15:11–32 contains the story of the most famous wanderer in Scripture—we want to answer some important questions about what really is going on in Jesus' parable about the prodigal son. Let's start with this one:

WHY DOES THE WILLFUL WANDERER LEAVE?

Who does that? Who gets up and walks away from their home, their family, and from everything that's familiar. Who abandons everything that protects, provides, and nourishes. What motivates such a person? Why does a wanderer depart? The possible answers are right here in the story Jesus told, though He probably didn't have a specific circumstance in mind. The story paralleled countless painful episodes He had seen. The account of this wanderer echoes a shocking number of real-life scenarios we've seen, too.

Jesus began, **"There was a man who had two sons. And the younger of them said to his father, 'Father, give me the share of property that is coming to me.' And he divided his property between them. Not many days later, the younger son gathered all he had and took a journey into a far country, and there he squandered his property in reckless living"** (vv. 11–13).

What set these events in motion is a matter of the will. The power to decide was felt and exercised. You will never understand the willful wanderer intellectually because his decisions don't make sense. His choices don't add up. You can't get your mind around his thought process. Maybe you are hoping to be able to say, "Oh, now I understand. This happened. And that happened. Then those resulted in this outcome. I get it." That clear insight is not going to happen. Willful wandering isn't really an intellectual thing. It's a matter of the will on autopilot: "It's my life. It's my vehicle. I'm driving. And that's the way it's going to be." At the root of a willful wanderer is this word—it's a big one—*control*. He or she is all about control. They may be headed over a cliff, but they are in control—that's what matters. Anything that threatens control is a problem for the willful wanderer. We can see that principle in the life of the prodigal.

Why does the willful wanderer leave? Here are three sample control issues:

• Authority threatens control.

Any authority threatens the person who has a huge issue with "I have to be in control." Notice how Jesus began: **"There was a man who had two sons."** John MacArthur has written a book called *A Tale of Two Sons* and Tim Keller has authored one entitled *Prodigal God*. Both of these excellent books focus on the second son—the one who never ran away; who thought his relationship with God was right because he was keeping the rules. In many senses, the older brother *is* Jesus' main focus here. He was talking to Pharisees who couldn't understand why Jesus would love sinners. So the older brother in the story represents the Pharisees.

Jesus actually told three stories of lost things in Luke 15, featuring sheep, coins, and finally, a lost son to make a point about God's heart for lost people. That's the main theme. But in the experience of the prodigal—the wanderer—we can learn a lot of specific lessons about relationships.

Jesus included the detail that the departing son was **"the younger."** It's not always the younger who's the prodigal. But in this instance, it was. Was he spoiled? Was he too protected? Was he the only planet in his universe? The bottom line is that we know that what he should have seen as a blessing, he saw as a burden. What he should have seen as provision and protection—his family, his father's authority—he saw as a problem. This is always the way with the willful wanderer. Any source of authority threatens control.

A teenage girl complains, "I'm driving my car along and a police officer stops me. I'm not happy about it because he's telling me I can't drive my car the way I want to drive it. Then my parents pile on and say, 'You be home—have the car in the driveway—by midnight.' Those are problems because I want to drive my car in my own way. I want to do what I want to do." Or a young man says, "I get called down to the principal's office at school. And he says, 'You parked your car in the wrong place.' And that's a problem to me because I don't want people telling me what to do."

How does an older prodigal sound? Your partner says to you, "I thought we had a marriage. You keep driving off. You do what you want to do." There really is no logic to it. But let anybody be in a position of authority to challenge the willful wanderer—that's going to be a problem. Authority threatens control.

It's interesting how Jesus unfolds the story at the end of verse 12. The younger son says, **"Father, give me the share of property that is coming to me."** Surprisingly, the father went along with the plan. Does that make sense to you? I'm thinking, "Hello, Dad! How about, *no*?!"

Everyone who's smiling and laughing at this point has never dealt with a willful wanderer. Refusal seems so obvious until you have faced off with someone determined to clash wills.

What you begin to learn with a willful opponent is that any assertion of authority makes conditions worse; resistance simply pushes them further away. The father really had no choice. It wasn't like the son was giving him an option.

You also have to realize what the son was asking for was boldly insulting. In Jesus' day and age, when parent-child relationships were very dignified, to say to your father, "I want my inheritance now," was really the same as saying, "I wish you were dead. You mean nothing to me. I want what you can give me. I'll take it now."

Even negotiating doesn't work with someone bent on control. You might suggest, "Couldn't we just give you a part of the farm and we'll build a dividing fence and you can call your side yours? You could put up your own cabin. Couldn't you just stay around?" Well, your plan would make sense if they didn't have huge control issues. Plus, their response reveals a second challenge:

• Proximity threatens control.

The last thing willful wanderers want is the beady eyes of authority looking at them all of the time. They cannot bear the possibility. In Jesus' story, even though the son had the money, he needed to leave. He had to get in his car and drive away. He had to put some space between him and anything that would threaten his control.

Luke 15:13 describes the departure. **"Not many days later . . ."** Not long after he got his inheritance, the younger son left.

The fact of "not many days" seems to indicate that the inheritance wasn't liquid (cash), so he probably fire-sold everything. The willful wanderer says, "I don't care how much I get. I just want the money. I'll cash out now," because they're not thinking about tomorrow, next year, or a decade from now—only about the next few moments. So he probably foolishly disposed of goods and property to get whatever money they would bring. **"Not many days later, the younger son gathered all he had."** If you've ever been in that father's position, it's very painful watching the willful wanderer pull out the suitcase and pack up the things. Dad asks, "Are you really going to do this?"

"Yes, I am!" he firmly says. And off he goes.

Why is he leaving? We want to yell, "Stop! Think! There's no future in this." But he is not thinking about the future. He's only thinking about "me" and "now."

Next Jesus said the young man went to **"a far country"** (v.13b). He had to get away from the person with the rules. He had to create distance from the place with control-threatening authority. But really, what he was trying to get away from was the rules themselves. Rules represent the third challenge as experienced by the willful wanderer:

• Policy threatens control.

The willful wanderer has his own declaration of independence: "Any system or rules designed to dictate to me that I cannot operate on the basis of my whims, I reject." Notice how quickly Jesus summarizes the course of events. **"He took**

a journey into a far country, and there he squandered his property in reckless living" (v. 13c). He wasted a sizeable stake. Literally, the language means he scattered it. He pulled into town and announced, "Hey everybody! The drinks are on me! Get me a room. Get me a woman." If asked, "How much do you want to spend?" the response was, "I don't care how much it costs! It's only money. Just get it for me right now!" His pockets were bursting with wealth and he foolishly squandered it.

Because he had never labored to get what he had, he didn't value it. He couldn't imagine his funds as a diminishing resource. He only saw it as something to spend lavishly.

If you could have joined him in that moment, he would have enthusiastically said to you, "Get in! I'm going for a ride!"

"Where are we headed?"

"I don't know! Get in!"

"Well, who's going with us?"

"I don't care. Get in! I'm driving!"

Such a person is so excited to have the apparent freedom "to do whatever I want to do," he can't see disaster rushing toward him. Freedom is an idol in the heart of the willful wanderer. Authority, proximity, and any form of policy threaten his wanton need for control.

At this point, the far country and lack of knowing are probably a merciful distance the willful wanderer's loved ones. His implosion is too painful to watch. Warning to the parents of a prodigal: don't try to bind him or her too close during this difficult season we pray will end, or the proximity may well destroy any possibility of a future. They are not in their right mind.

You might ask, "Why does someone hate rules so much?" These three answers will help:

(1) The hate flows from a lack of faith. They don't believe God's rules are good for their protection. They won't trust His character, and they resent His intrusion.

(2) The hate reveals a lack of humility. They are too prideful or stubborn to admit when they are wrong. You might suggest, "A few people have done what you're doing. It didn't work out too well for them. Would you like to hear their stories?"

"No! Absolutely not" is their answer.

(3) The hate for the rules is compensation for a lack of self-control. At the end of the day the reasonableness of the rules is not important to a person who's driven by autonomous desire. "I need to control things, so I'm blind to my lack of faith, lack of humility, and lack of self-control. I'm blind to these realities." The willful wanderer has a condition called—this is an old German word we don't use much anymore—*wanderlust*. Wanderlust is the desire to be on the road; to be moving; to be somewhere new; to leave all restraints behind. Many people can look to a time in their life where they made bad decisions prompted by wanderlust. "Yeah, I did that. I had to go. I had to see. I wanted to be on the move." That's the point.

Why does the willful wanderer leave? It's about control.

Jesus' story has a great ending—in His time. It comes to a good conclusion. Let's move to this question we all ponder:

WHEN DOES THE WILLFUL WANDERER COME HOME?

As a pastor, I hear versions of this question far too often. When is she coming home? When is my husband going to finally figure it out? When will I get the call from the bus station? Will he knock or slip in the back door?

In God's time he's going to figure it out, the call will come, the soft knock will echo down the hallway. But let's look at some of the circumstances God uses to bring about a return. Circumstances are going to have to break the will of the wanderer. Not arguments. Not proof of the foolishness or the danger. Not arguments (in case you didn't think I meant it the first time). Not tearful appeals—"How can you not have compassion for your children? How can you not see what your choices are doing to us?" Not arguments (in case you skipped over the two previous). Not power plays, forced conformity, or getting your wanderer into a corner of common sense.

Here's when the willful wanderer comes home. The car has to explode. The hammer has to fall. That's the way it really is. The crushing and merciless weight of reality is the most effective means to bring the willful wanderer home. And not before. So don't get between the hammer and the work. God's got to do it. God has to bring the person to their knees. Make sure that you're not nourishing or supporting some artificial sense of well-being when they really need the train to come off the rails.

People sometimes tell me, "James, it's kind of funny the way you describe what brings a willful wanderer to his or her senses.

Obviously you don't mean a car or train crash. So what do you mean?"

Well let's get some examples from the text. Here's the first one:

• **Pockets must be empty.**

When the money runs out, reality starts setting in. That's the first hint of trouble. Notice verse 14, **"And when he had spent everything."** When's he coming home? The wallet and bank account were empty. Credit cards were maxed out. He had nothing left. I take the Bible literally, so when Jesus says *everything*, I don't think he was down to a few bucks. He didn't have a quarter, dime, nickel, or a penny. He was flat broke. "When he had spent everything."

Family life in those days was tied to property ownership. To get his inheritance early—a third of the entire estate—he had torn his family apart. But now his formerly full pockets were empty. In the past, he would have turned to his family to bail him out. Now the wanderer needs what he previously rejected. He needs what he left in the dust.

Notice that three things had changed:

(1) He had less. We know he had spent *everything*.

(2) There was less to be had. Suddenly life was hardship, because **"a severe famine arose in that country"** (v. 14). Times got tough. God was ordering all the circumstances—in His time—to bring the willful wanderer to the end of himself. So he had less, but there was less to be had. The difficulties

weren't just internal to him, they were also circumstantial. He had nothing, and the economy was in shambles.

(3) He felt like he had been had. All of his friends had been right there whooping it up with him, but now the text seems to indicate his companions were only along for the ride and bailed before the crash. His brother's bitter accusation later is, he **"devoured your property with prostitutes"** (v. 30). We don't know the details of his **"reckless living"** (v. 13) but we can guess. Apparently there was a sexual component to it. We all know the excesses that partying can lead to. I'm sure it was all-of-the-above living that vaporized the funds. But when the money ran out and the economy tanked and the friends vanished, all that was left was the lonely reality of the end of the road!

Are you a willful wanderer? Do you find yourself at the place where your formerly full pockets are way empty? You thought you had so much and it would last so long. How's life going for you now? Where has that plan left you? What do you have left you can be sure about? It's not what you thought, is it? It's not as good. It's not as fun. It's not as free. Satan promises freedom and gives bondage, slavery, addiction, devastation, and disease. He's a liar! And the only thing worse than falling for his lies is falling for them for a lifetime. Realizing the lies is a call to the willful wanderer to come home!

- **Party must be ended.**

If we could intervene in this boy's life between verses 14 and 15, we would probably say, "Dude! Come home right now!"

But he's still fighting for control. Instead of coming home, he tries to fund his own party. Jesus continued, **"So he went and hired himself out"** (v. 15). I'm sure his dad and brother would have said in unison, "You got a *what*? A *job*?" This kid probably hadn't worked a day in his life. He's about to discover the reality of no skills in the marketplace.

The son who ran away was probably between eighteen and twenty years old or he wouldn't have gotten the inheritance. He certainly wouldn't have been able to travel to an out-of-the-zip-code, out-of-the-state place, or to a different country. He was a foreigner in a **"far country"** (v. 13). His age, background, and experience added up to one conclusion: he was not super hirable.

Notice the job that he got. **"So he went and hired himself out to one of the citizens of that country, who sent him into his fields to feed pigs"** (v. 15). It's almost impossible for us living in North America in this century to comprehend what went off in the minds of a Jewish audience when they heard that this Jewish young man was feeding pigs. The Jewish people were forbidden to eat pork. Actually, the rabbis taught: "Cursed is anyone who breeds swine." Jews weren't allowed to feed pigs; they certainly weren't permitted to raise them. When Jesus got to this point of the story, there must have been a significant reaction from the audience. This boy was doing the unthinkable!

Slopping pigs is not just any farm job. There was a hog farm down the road from my grandmother's farm. I remember as a kid driving out each Sunday to dinner at my grandma's house. On the way my dad would say every week, "Roll up the windows. Crank them tight!" Now, I know that different manure produces different fragrances. You can smell a variety of odors on livestock farms. But most people agree there's no comparison between cattle manure and pig manure when it comes to offending the senses. Pigs produce their own unique stench. They create a mess and then root, wallow, and sleep in it! Hog lifestyle adds to the problem. The young man in Jesus' story found himself in the middle of this scene. Picture him struggling under a type of yoke over his shoulders that supported two heavy pails of slop. And he's walking among the pigs, scooping feed that only a pig would look at. The party is now officially over.

Let's interview him. "Young man, how's your day going?"

"Not great. I'm a Jewish boy in a foreign country. I used to be rich. I spent everything. Now I feed pigs. That's what I do." Is he broken? Close. Is he coming home? Not yet. The stronger the will, the further the wanderer must go to get to the end.

Before the willful wanderer comes home, the pockets must be empty and the party must be ended. This sets the stage for the third key discovery:

- **Poverty must be experienced.**

Until this moment, the young man could have said, "I'm learning responsibility. I've got a job. I'm still in control." That would be before a few days on the job. He is about to experience poverty as almost no one growing up in a North American context has ever experienced—in terms of a world standard—

true poverty. Even people living on welfare in our society are nowhere close to poverty by a world standard. A prodigal has to discover firsthand the reality of authentic poverty. They have to experience it.

Here is the young man's breaking point. His boss **"sent him into his fields to feed pigs. And he was longing to be fed with the pods that the pigs ate"** (vv. 15–16). He was so hungry, he was willing to put his face in filth to satisfy his hunger. Now that's poverty up close and personal. The willful wanderer never saw this coming. He was so protected and so provided for in his sheltered upbringing that it never really occurred to him nor did he have any basis for understanding what was really out there in this world.

So off he went to join the stream of willful wanderers through history. Like the one who walked away from his marriage and his family. Or the one who left her parents and siblings behind in order to exercise control to experience freedom—the great idol—but ultimately to experience humiliation, shame, and the end of the road. He chose to sin; he chose to suffer.

Here comes the reality of poverty. The willful wanderer is the fool who never fears until he falls. The willful wanderer is the rebel who never rests until he hits rock bottom. The willful wanderer is not coming home until she is carrying a framed certificate as a graduate from the School of Hard Knocks. Been there; done that; have the memories. The indelible experience is what she is bringing with her. "I get it. I get it!" She is not coming back until she does. In His time.

Poverty must be experienced. Jesus' description of the moment includes this insight, **"he was longing"** (v. 16). What should have been loathsome to him he lusted after. What was waste to others he badly wanted. That is a picture of poverty. His desperation breaks his will.

Please let me speak for a moment to anyone who knows they fit in Jesus' story. Listen, willful wanderer; listen, prodigal son or daughter or spouse; listen, stubborn young adult who hangs around the fringes of the church but daily and weekly feeds from the trough of the pigs' food of this world—are you ready yet? Are you ready yet to admit the escape hasn't given you what you thought it would give? Are you ready to say, "I've wandered far enough; I don't want this anymore. I can see where this is going and I don't want to go there." Are you ready to pull up short, turn back, humble your stubborn heart, and say to God and to your family and your church, "I want a change in my life; I want something different; it's not what I thought; I want what I had; I want to come home"? Here's my warning: your pockets must be empty, the party's got to be over, you have to really know what poverty is, or you won't be able to come home. If you think you're ready to come home, pray about that list in your life.

Now back to those who *haven't* gone the way of the wanderer. You might ask, "But is there really hope for a person like you have been describing? Can they actually come home? Can a willful wanderer really change?"

YES! Absolutely. I have heard the reports. I've seen the evidence. I can bear witness to people I know who can say, "I was a total prodigal! Against all odds, God brought me home." Absolutely, wanderers can return! God Himself is in the process of reaching them for that very purpose.

But here is the exact turning point: they have to *repent*. That's the biblical word. They have to repent—to turn away from sin and toward God. They have to undergo true change. Actually, the story of the prodigal son is a case study in God's methods. The prodigal is the poster boy for genuine repentance. Let's look closely at the process behind our next question:

HOW DOES THE WILLFUL WANDERER REPENT?

For those who have welcomed a willful wanderer home, the process of his or her repentance is often a mystery. It's worth listening closely to his or her descriptions of the turning moment, for we may never have a closer glimpse of God at work in someone's life. Fortunately, Jesus' story provides us with God's approach.

- **The mind awakens to reality.**

When we were last with the prodigal, he was hip-deep in a pig wallow, considering the menu before him. **"And he was longing to be fed with the pods that the pigs ate, and no one gave him anything. But when he came to himself . . ."** (vv. 16–17). That's the awakening moment right there, and it happens in a split second. It really does. The lightbulb goes on. NASB translates that last phrase, **"when he came to his**

senses." The realization was sudden and painful: "What am I *doing*? Sin doesn't satisfy. Selfishness doesn't work."

Now two things have to come together for the lightbulb to go on—the mind awakened to reality. The immediate condition of the prodigal can be described this way: he is finally without *means* and without *inclination*. As long as they still have *means*, prodigals will try something else stupid. They must run out of ways to get in further trouble. If they have *inclination*, they're still on the road. They have to be able to not want it (control, autonomy, the last word) anymore; they "had it, don't want it." When the means is gone and the inclination has left, there's going to be a wake-up moment. There's going to be a snap back to reality.

Here is an important caution for the rest of us. Despite his sudden discovery of the obvious, we ought not to be harsh with the willful wanderer. Do you slap blind people for not seeing? If you were walking down a road and you bumped into a blind person, would you slap him and say, "Watch where you're going!" I hope you would not do that. Prodigals—through their own fault, but nevertheless—have poked out their own eyes. They can't see. They flat out can't see the truth. Rhetoric will not open their eyes. But when the party is over and the poverty is experienced, they're going to come to their senses. The reality of their desperate condition will suddenly appear. They're going to get it in an instant.

Several hundred years ago, John Newton, himself a notorious wanderer, wrote a song for prodigals:

Amazing grace,
How sweet the sound
That saved a wretch like me.
I once was lost,
But now I'm found.
Was **blind** but now I see.

As if waking up, the wanderer says, "I get it. I didn't get it an hour ago. But now I *see* it!" That's the moment. And here in Jesus' story, the first part of repentance is that prodigal's mind awakening to reality.

At this point, I expect some pushback. People hear this story and say, "Blind? Okay. But why can't they just see it? They're on the wrong road! Why don't they notice what's happening?"

It's worth taking a moment to break that "blindness" down a little bit.

(1) Their clock is broken.

Most of us have a sense of time. We're not just thinking about today. We think about tomorrow, next week, and a month or year from now. We know that decisions we make today will affect the future. We are used to thinking about down the road. The prodigal doesn't. Their clock is stopped on right now. They struggle to think fifteen minutes from now. "What am I doing tonight? I don't know." Any forethought is a huge leap for the willful wanderer. They live in the moment. Their clock is broken.

(2) Their compass is busted.

I hope you have been to the Grand Canyon. Pictures don't do it justice. It's very cool; get there. I've got to be honest; I've always liked jumping off cliffs into water. Heights don't bother me. But when I got to the Grand Canyon, I didn't run up to the edge to see the sight. A few feet from the lip I slowed down a bit. And when I got right to the edge, I was very careful.

Not the willful wanderer; his compass is completely broken. He doesn't know where he is or how close to the edge he has come. A prodigal doesn't sense the danger coming. As I've said already: the fool is the person who doesn't fear until he falls. The Scripture says, **"There is a way that seems right to a man, but its end is the way to death."**[1] The wanderer's compass and clock are broken. But those aren't their only handicaps.

(3) Their senses—let's call that their computer—are malfunctioning.

Wanderers are not in their right mind. Your mind sees, smells, hears, and senses things. It rights thinking, records and compares experiences, and learns from mistakes. The willful wanderer—his entire operating system is broken. It's not working properly. So he has to have a crash.

The experience of the willful prodigal reminds me of a sight I saw recently from the glassed-in walkway between two buildings on one of our church campuses. I looked out the window and down below was a bird lying in the grass. If it wasn't dead, it was definitely stunned. Apparently this feathered creature had been having an awesome day. "Just look at this sweet place I can fly between these two buildings." Brrrrrrr. BAM! It didn't notice the window. That was the end of that. One second before impact that bird was thinking, "I am AWESOME!" BAM! And it's over. That's what happens to the willful wanderer. "I'm free! I'm in control! I am awesome!" BAM! And they awake. For the young man in Jesus' story it was the moment he thought, "I was going to eat that?! I was so insane!" Instead, he came to his senses and the light went on. The mind awakened to reality; but, that's only the first step.

- **Will submits to reality.**

The young man begins to assess his situation, rethinking where he came from. His reasoning gets very practical: **"How many of my father's hired servants have more than enough bread?"** (v. 17). Good thinking. "Hired servants" were the day workers. They didn't even belong to the household. During harvest the father would go into the marketplace and say, "Does anybody want a job? We've got some extra work." He would bring them in and give them cash at the end of the day. Even those guys got enough from his generous father. So he draws some preliminary conclusions: **"How many of my father's hired servants have more than enough bread, but I perish here with hunger!"**

Now we see the wanderer's will engaging with the new reality. **"I will arise"** (v. 18). That's a great moment. It's a turning around and it's happening in God's timing. **"I will arise and go to my father, and I will say to him, 'Father, I have sinned against heaven and before you'"** (v. 18). When there's real repentance, there's also an awareness of how my sin affects God and others. The thing the prodigal couldn't see is now incredibly obvious. His mind has awakened to reality and his will submits to it.

The prodigal says, "I'm going to go home. I'm going to tell my father I was wrong and cast myself on his mercy. He treats slaves better than I'm being treated here." His will forms a plan of action. That step is really important.

In 2 Corinthians 7, Paul's teaching on repentance helpfully shows us how not to mistake regret for repentance. It's not enough for us to simply *feel bad* for the mess we've created. Paul wrote:

> **As it is, I rejoice, not because you were grieved, but because you were grieved into repenting. For you felt a godly grief, so that you suffered no loss through us. For godly grief produces a repentance that leads to salvation without regret, whereas worldly grief produces death.** [2]

Worldly repentance is regret: "Sorry I got caught. Sorry I look bad. Sorry I feel bad. Sorry I've upset you. Sorry I—" Worldly sorrow doesn't drive us from death but toward it. That's not repentance.

When this young man says, **"I have sinned against heaven and before you. I am no longer worthy to be called your son,"** (vv. 18–19) that's repentance. He came to his senses; that's his mind. **"I will arise . . . I will go"**; that's his will submitting to reality.

One other aspect of the prodigal's experience needs to be engaged:

- **Emotions conform to reality.**

Up to a few days before, the prodigal had taken all the great things about his life for granted. He demanded his inheritance without a hint of gratitude. Now reality has given him the news that he deserves nothing. He has decided to return home, but he isn't assuming he can resume his place. He knows he must admit, **"I am no longer worthy to be called your son"** (v. 21).

Is that true? It is absolutely true. He *isn't* worthy. What he said and did forfeited his right to be treated as a son.

Considering that young man's situation, aren't you glad that in God's family we don't operate on rights? God didn't treat us as we deserved to be treated. This kid deserved nothing and he knew it! Yet that's why the kingdom of God is so *awesome*—because he's going to get everything he doesn't deserve and he's not going to get what he does deserve—just like us. It's called God's grace and mercy.

The prodigal's thoughts reveal one of the things the willful wanderer is concerned about. "If I admit who I really am—if I acknowledge what I've really done—what kind of reception will I get?"

Here's the reception that the willful wanderer will get from God Himself, because the father in this story represents God the Father. The first message I ever preached at Harvest, day one—was called "The Day God Ran." In all of Scripture, we only see God running one time. He doesn't run to church. He doesn't run to the mission field. But He runs to a repentant sinner. That's what Jesus' story is all about.

Once the prodigal made his decision, he made his way home. **"And he arose and came to his father"** (v. 20). It wasn't just a thought process; he actually did it—another indication of true repentance. **"And he arose and came to his father. But while he was still a long way off . . ."** Isn't that the way it really is back where he came from? The wanderer hasn't even been thinking about home, but things there have never been right since he left. But this father—there was no way in the world he saw this kid a long way off unless he was going every day and *looking*. He was scanning the horizon and longing for the return of the son he loved. All of the hopes . . . all of the dreams . . . all of the plans . . . all of the prayers—it was all for this day. The father was anticipating the time when the willful wanderer would fall to his knees, admit he was wrong, and come back to what he had so foolishly left.

The waiting father did more than *see* his son. **"But while he was still a long way off, his father saw him and felt compassion."** I love that word *compassion*. It means *to feel for the other person*. Instead of any hint of rejection, punishment, conditions, or hesitance to receive the wanderer back, the father's heart reaches for him even long before his feet begin to move. That's God's heart, instantly and overwhelmingly responsive to the repentant sinner. Likewise, God's authentic people always reflect His heart.

Even before the son made his speech, the father felt what the son was feeling. What would the son have been feeling? Ashamed. Embarrassed. Foolish in the extreme, not to mention latent feelings of filth from his recent hog farm job. He was in a far country and had no money, so he walked home. He had days and weeks—maybe months—to work on his speech. He thought about it, every step taking him closer to the meeting that he couldn't get out of his mind. He probably hadn't showered. He may have tried to wash up a little bit, but he was in filthy clothes. He had no shoes on. He smelled like where he worked. He came as he was, rehearsing his speech: "This is how it worked out, Dad. I was so sure, but I was *so* wrong. I was so determined, but I was so twisted." Trudging over the last hill, he was ready for the moment of truth.

What he wasn't ready for was seeing his father running toward him! He tried to get the words out, but his father was all over him. Jesus said the father **"embraced and kissed him"** (v. 20). Dad threw his arms around him and (the phrase means) *kissed him repeatedly*; all over—on the face and on the neck; and held on to him, no doubt weeping for joy.

Picture this moment and consider how those roles have played out in your life: **"But while he was still a long way off, his father saw him and felt compassion, and ran and embraced him and kissed him. And the son said to him, 'Father, I have sinned against heaven and before you. I am no longer worthy to be called your son.'"**[3] The son came home. Reader, have you come home? Have you been reading these pages, weeping for a loved one you long to open the door for? Don't miss this last part of the story.

WILLFUL WANDERER, COME HOME

Wanderers of each of the types we've looked at in this book have a question. Perhaps the willful wanderer, realizing the extent of his destructive actions, asks it most desperately: What will I find when I come home? Jesus tells us God's answer to that question in His story. If we are going to take seriously the command to go get the wanderer, we had better be prepared to follow God's lead in the reception we give to those who come home. Here are God's answers:

- **You will find a healing embrace.**

You are welcomed with a hug like no other. The father overwhelmed the son with his embrace and kisses. You come home to the sense in the arms of God the Father that you are loved with an everlasting love and that *nothing* **"will be able to separate [you] from the love of God,"**[4] no matter where you've been or no matter what you've done. God loves you. He wants you home. You come to a healing embrace.

- **You will find a total forgiveness.**

"And the son said to him . . ." Here's the speech—so well-rehearsed: **"Father, I have sinned against heaven and before you. I am no longer worthy to be called your son"** (v. 21). The father, however, will not even enter into that discussion. Instead, **"The father said to his servants . . ."** (v. 22). He didn't even answer the son. "My statement has already been made in my embrace and my kisses." This is the moment when we finally begin to understand Romans 8:32, **"He who did not spare his**

own Son but gave him up for us all, how will he not also with him graciously give us all things?"

The son was still trying to get through his speech while his dad began to issue orders: **"But the father said to his servants, 'Bring quickly the best robe, and put it on him, and put a ring on his hand (a family symbol), and shoes on his feet.' "** (v. 22). "Quick! Bless and refresh him. He's home, let's make him look the part! He doesn't owe me anything. I'm not looking to get. I want to give more now that he's ready to receive. I've been longing for this." Those statements are total welcome and restoration. What a beautiful picture of forgiveness.

- **You will find a celebration of your return.**

Luke 15:23 continues the father's commands: **"And bring the fattened calf."** A family with means would always have on hand an animal raised for a festive occasion. The father has been planning for a special event. "Bring it! . . . **'and let us eat and celebrate.' "** It's time.

Don't ever wonder how God the Father feels when a wanderer comes home. All of Luke 15 is about the celebration that goes on in heaven, about all the work and prayer behind the scenes to make the moment of humility and return possible. You can bless the heart of God. You can kick off a true party in your honor, willful wanderer. Come home to a celebration of your return. Finally.

- **You will find a future filled with hope.**

The father's words over his returned son ought to take

our breath away. **"For this my son was dead . . ."** Dad had thought, "It was over; he was gone; he wasn't coming back. I almost lost hope." The departure of a willful wanderer does feel like a death in the family! **" . . . And is alive again."** His return was like a resurrection. **"He was lost** (he was gone), **and is found"** (v. 24). The wanderer is alive and found, with a future filled with hope. What a welcome to come home to!

TO THE WANDERER

Much of this chapter (and the book) has necessarily focused on comfort and understanding for the family of the willful wanderer. But its highest objective and purpose is for you, the wanderer. If you have read this far, I have to believe you would honestly say, "I've made choices I should not have made and they took me places I did not want to go." And if you can say those words, what would keep *you* from coming home—first to God your Father, and then to those who love you?

Sin will always cost more than we want to pay. It will always bring us to poverty in ways we never imagined. Whatever your previous impression, the true church of Jesus Christ is filled with loving people who have been in the place where you are now. I have been there. I could take you to a place in a Bible in my office where a date is written: a day; a month; a year when I knew the right but found myself far from it. I've had to respond to an invitation like I'm about to give you right now.

Wanderer, maybe you've never really given your life to Christ; never really given Him the wheel. But today you want to come home to the God who loves you, who sent His Son to pay for your sin. Or, maybe you're like me on that day so long ago. You've known the truth but you've been living apart from it. In some way, God knows you know. And you need to have a turning and a returning. I want to challenge you not to miss this opportunity to come home.

You are one courageous decision away from the most important turn in your life. I don't know when you're going to have another opportunity like this. So if God is stirring truth in your heart, have courage and make a change. The Bible says all of heaven rejoices, not over ninety-nine people who do not see how poorly they are doing, but over one who truly repents. Jesus said, "**I tell you, there will be more joy in heaven over one sinner who repents than over ninety-nine righteous persons who need no repentance.**"[5] God the Father is ready to throw a party in your honor if you will tell Him with your mouth and life that you are ready to come home. Let me close this chapter by offering a prayer for you.

Father, thank You. Thank You for Your Word. Thank You for this place where this reader finds herself or himself in this moment. Thank You for how You work in our lives. I thank You that You give grace to the humble. Thank You for opening the mind and eyes of this wanderer to see they are far from where they want to be. Thank You for stirring in them a longing for home.

Thank You that Your grace is rushing upon this precious one right now. God, we have been where they are. We don't judge them. But we know what the answer is. And we thank You they're finding it—in You. We pray that You would give them great mercy and forgiveness.

Thank You that You are the Lord, **"slow to anger and abounding in steadfast love and faithfulness."**[6]

We pray today that You would help this wanderer to sense Your presence; that You would minister to them; that You would cause this to be a turning point in their life.

How could it be, God, that in a moment, a life could be changed? But our lives have been changed in such a moment. And a course can be corrected and a direction can be set and things can be left behind.

Thank You for the promise: **"Therefore, if anyone is in Christ, he is a new creation. The old has passed away; behold, the new has come."**[7] I pray that that would be the experience of this wanderer today. In Jesus' name, Amen.

GO GET THE

WANDERER

·

IF YOU ARE FAMILIAR with the parable of the prodigal, you may have come to the end of the last chapter and wondered, "What about the older brother? What's his story?"

His story is found in Luke 15:25–32:

Now his older son was in the field, and as he came and drew near to the house, he heard music and dancing. And he called one of the servants and asked what these things meant.

And he said to him, "Your brother has come, and your father has killed the fattened calf, because he has received him back safe and sound."

But he was angry and refused to go in. His father came out and entreated him, but he answered his father, "Look, these many years I have served you, and I never

disobeyed your command, yet you never gave me a young goat, that I might celebrate with my friends. But when this son of yours came, who has devoured your property with prostitutes, you killed the fattened calf for him!"

And he said to him, "Son, you are always with me, and all that is mine is yours. It was fitting to celebrate and be glad, for this your brother was dead, and is alive; he was lost, and is found."

Let's be truthful in closing. Some of us find it tempting to resent the return of the prodigal. It's not exactly the fact that they come back that bothers us; it's all the fun we think they got away with that really works on our minds. But it's easy to envy the fun and miss the high price they have paid and are paying for their wandering.

It's even easier for us to miss the danger of becoming a wanderer who never left home. Clearly, all those years of staying at home didn't result in the older brother gaining his father's heart. They have lived different lives under the same roof, the older son resenting his role instead of joining his father in heartfelt concern for his brother, anticipating his return, and rejoicing at the sight of him cresting the hill in the distance. How much better if father and son had come running together to meet the prodigal!

If you know and are hurting in any way because of a prodigal, ask God to eliminate in you any desire to resist or reject the homecoming of that wanderer. Ask Him to give you the father's heart in this story, filled with compassion and genuine welcome. Even more, as you wait for your prodigal to return, ask God for wisdom in recognizing how you might be involved in finding other wanderers and inviting them to come home.

Jesus dealt with prodigals in His own family. John 7:5 tells us, **"For not even his brothers believed in him."** We don't know much about how Jesus approached this heartache, but He let them have their way. After the resurrection, 1 Corinthians 15:7 tells us, He appeared to James, his half-brother. He went and got that wanderer. James went from not believing in his brother to becoming a leader in the church in Jerusalem! When he came home, he came all the way. Eventually two of Jesus' half-brothers contributed to the New Testament (James and Jude).

We are back where we started with James 5:19–20. Because Jesus went to get him, James knew firsthand what it was like to wander from the truth and then come home. Perhaps that's why James closed his letter with those words, and I'll do the same with this book: **"My brothers, if anyone among you wanders from the truth and someone brings him back, let him know that whoever brings back a sinner from his wandering will save his soul from death and will cover a multitude of sins."**

Father, thank You for the good work You always do in our lives, right up to that day of our final homecoming! Continue to change us as Your people. Make us always a place and a people who long for and look for and seek the wanderer. Make us faithful sowers of the seed of the gospel and the grace of Your invitation, even to those who have wandered from the truth, to come home. All these things we pray in the strong name of Jesus, Amen.

NOTES

Chapter One: Go Get the Wanderer

1. John 9:2–3
2. James 5:16
3. James 5:17–18
4. Hebrews 11:25
5. John 14:6
6. 1 Timothy 3:15
7. Matthew 9:36
8. Luke 15:7
9. KJV
10. Luke 15:32

Chapter Two: Fearful Wanderer—Come Home!

1. Matthew 26:14–16
2. Matthew 26:33
3. 1 Corinthians 10:12
4. Jeremiah 6:15 and 8:12
5. Luke 15:7
6. Exodus 34:6

Chapter Three: Doubtful Wanderer—Come Home!

1. John 20:24–29
2. John 18:38
3. John 9:36
4. Norman Geisler, *I Don't Have Enough Faith to Be an Atheist* (Wheaton, IL: Crossway, 2004).
5. James MacDonald, *God Wrote a Book* (Wheaton, IL: Crossway, 2004).
6. Psalm 19:1
7. Ecclesiastes 3:11
8. 2 Chronicles 15:2
9. Job 2:10
10. Matthew 5:45
11. 2 Peter 3:9
12. Acts 16:31
13. Matthew 5:10–12
14. Matthew 5:44 NKJV
15. Matthew 18:21–35
16. 2 Thessalonians 1:6
17. NKJV
18. Psalm 139:7
19. John 20:19–22
20. John 11:16 italics added
21. John 20:19
22. NKJV
23. Matthew 9:29
24. John 20:25
25. John 20:26
26. Mark 9:24

Chapter Four: Sensual Wanderer—Come Home!

1. Known for this phrase, Postman wrote a book in 1985 entitled *Amusing Ourselves to Death: Public Discourse in the Age of Show Business.* Reissued in 2005, it is still considered a masterpiece of critique of an entertainment/information-glutted society.
2. 1 Corinthians 6:12 KJV
3. Judges 13:24

4. Judges 14:1
5. Judges 14:14
6. Luke 15:11–32
7. Romans 13:14

Chapter Five: Willful Wanderer—Come Home!

1. Proverbs 14:12
2. 2 Corinthians 7:9
3. Luke 15:20
4. Romans 8:39
5. Luke 15:7
6. Exodus 34:6
7. 2 Corinthians 5:17

ABOUT THE AUTHOR

 James MacDonald (D. Min. Phoenix Seminary) has committed his life to the unapologetic proclamation of God's Word. He is the founding senior pastor of Harvest Bible Chapel, one of the fastest growing churches in the Chicago area, reaching over 13,000 lives each weekend. Through James' leadership and by God's grace, a church-planting ministry was formed in 2002, *Harvest Bible Fellowship*, which has planted more than 85 churches across North America and around the world. James also teaches on *Walk in the Word*, a daily radio broadcast committed to "igniting passion in the people of God through the proclamation of truth." James is the author of several books including *Lord Change My Attitude, When Life is Hard, Always True, Vertical Church*, and most recently, *Authentic*. James and his wife, Kathy, have three adult children and make their home in suburban Chicago. You can find out more about James and his ministries at WalkintheWord.com.

OTHER TITLES
YOU MAY ENJOY

978-0-8024-5724-0

Root out the hypocrisy. Authenticity is not copied or fake. It's about the basics. Simple. Truth. Transparency. Authentic. Developing the disciplines of a sincere faith.

OTHER TITLES
YOU MAY ENJOY

978-0-8024-5870-4

When life is hard, when things get ugly, when all hope seems to be lost ... that is when we are able to display the superiority of the life lived in God.

Working his way through five questions we've all asked, James MacDonald helps us understand what we should do now.

Also available as an ebook

MOODY
Publishers™

From the Word to Life

www.MoodyPublishers.com

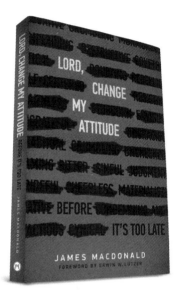

OTHER TITLES
YOU MAY ENJOY

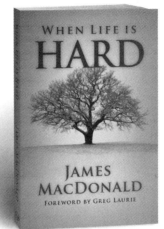

978-0-8024-5870-4

When life is hard, when things get ugly, when all hope seems to be lost … that is when we are able to display the superiority of the life lived in God.

Working his way through five questions we've all asked, James MacDonald helps us understand what we should do now.

Also available as an ebook

MOODY
Publishers™

From the Word to Life

www.MoodyPublishers.com

MORE BESTSELLERS FROM
JAMES MACDONALD
AND MOODY PUBLISHERS

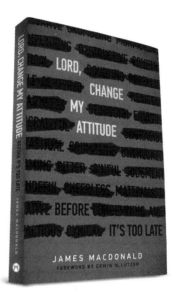

978-0-8024-1319-2

"You can stop the flow of negativity that causes happiness to hemorrhage, and you can start the flow of good attitudes that cause abundant joy to abound."

—James MacDonald

While we can't change our attitudes overnight, we can recognize wrong attitudes and begin working on right attitudes.

Also available as an ebook

MOODY
Publishers™

From the Word to Life

www.MoodyPublishers.com